The Prophet's Mandate

By Lisa Sims

ISBN: 9781736705704

© 2021 Lisa Sims

All rights reserved.

No part of this publication may be reproduced, stored in a retrieval system or transmitted in any form or by any means, electronic, mechanical, photocopying, recording or otherwise, without prior permission of the publisher.

Scriptures taken from the New King James Version®.
Copyright © 1982 by Thomas Nelson, Inc. Used by permission. All rights reserved.

Scripture quotations taken from the Amplified® Bible (AMP), Copyright © 2015 by The Lockman Foundation. Used by permission. All rights reserved.

Published by Lams Publishing

Contents

	Introduction...	5
1	Three Types of Prophets...............................	7
2	What is Prophecy?..	18
3	Prophecy is Important to God.......................	30
4	God the Revealer: The Prophet the Revelator.....	34
5	Prophetic Protocol..	62
6	Methods of Prophesying...............................	67
7	Prophetic Worship..	76
8	A Company of Prophets................................	89
9	The Prophet's Mandate.................................	94
10	Old Testament Prophets...............................	109
11	Jezebel: The Destroyer of Prophets..............	129
12	Myths regarding prophets and Prophecies....	145
13	Waging War With Prophecies.......................	150
14	Prophetic Teams & Prophetic Presbytery.....	160
15	The Prophet's Authority................................	165
16	Prophetic Interpretation................................	172
	About the Author..	176

Introduction

This book is aimed to propel you into fulfilling God's mandate for the prophet. There is also a Q & A section at the end of each chapter for you to complete.

A prophet can be a male or female. However, in this book, the prophet will be referred to as "he" and "him". This in no way implies that all prophets are male. It is simply done to make it easier to write and read this book. .

The Prophet's Mandate reveals God's mandate for the prophet, one of which is to speak exactly what God says without compromise. God is restoring the type of Old Testament prophets who were holy and feared God, and who prophesied without compromising and with tremendous accuracy. They were bold and fearless. Along with exercising the office of the prophet, they were also taught the rudiments of secular knowledge. These prophets preached pure morality and the heartfelt worship of Jehovah. They worked with the priesthood and monarchy in guiding the state right and checking all attempts at illegality and tyranny (Easton's Bible Dictionary, 2021). The Old Testament prophets were holy, on fire for God, detailed and accurate.

The Prophet's Mandate is aimed at raising up this type of Old Testament prophet and releasing and activating a company of end time prophets that will go into their market places, churches, nations and other places to release the true prophetic word of the Lord with accurate detail- prophecies that will transform lives, organizations, Churches, nations, monarchs, entities, presidents and other heads of state.

Chapter 1
Three Types of Prophetic People

The Prophet is one of the five - fold ministry governmental offices of apostles, prophets, teachers, evangelists and pastors. These men and women of God are gifts to the body of Christ. The five-fold ministry gifts are called to train, equip and edify the body of Christ. When Jesus ascended to heaven after he completed his ministry on the earth, which was to die for the sins of all mankind, he gave gifts to men. His purpose for doing so is very clearly outlined in the word of God.

> **Ephesians 4: 8, 11-16**
> [8]"When He ascended on high, He led captivity captive, And gave gifts to men." [11] And He Himself gave some to be apostles, some prophets, some evangelists, and some pastors and teachers, [12] for the equipping of the saints for the work of ministry, for the [a]edifying of the body of Christ, [13] till we all come to the unity of the faith and of the knowledge of the Son of God, to a perfect man, to the measure of the stature of the fullness of Christ; [14] that we should no longer be children, tossed to and fro and carried about with every wind of doctrine, by the trickery of men, in the cunning craftiness of deceitful plotting, [15] but, speaking the truth in love, may grow up in all things into Him who is the head—Christ— [16] from whom the whole body, joined and knit together by what every joint supplies, according to the effective working by which every part does its share, causes growth of the body for the edifying of itself in love.

The prophet, along with the apostle, teacher, evangelist and pastor, is called to train, equip and edify the body of Christ. The five-fold ministry gifts hold governmental positions in the body of Christ. Just as there are ranks in the military, there are ranks in the Kingdom of God and in the body of Christ. The five-fold ministry gifts carry the highest ranks in the Kingdom of God. The prophet ranks second in the body of Christ after the apostle.

1 Cor. 12: 28
And God has appointed these in the church: first apostles, second prophets, third teachers, after that miracles, then gifts of healings, helps, administrations, varieties of tongues.

The prophet is part of the foundation of the Church, and Jesus is the chief cornerstone.

Eph. 2: 20-22.
[19] Now, therefore, you are no longer strangers and foreigners, but fellow citizens with the saints and members of the household of God, [20] having been built on the foundation of the apostles and prophets, Jesus Christ Himself being the chief corner*stone,* [21] in whom the whole building, being fitted together, grows into a holy temple in the Lord, [22] in whom you also are being built together for a dwelling place of God in the Spirit.

The foundation of a natural building gets stepped on continually. So too do prophets get "stepped on". The term "stepped on" means to treat someone badly. Prophets are often stepped on (treated badly) by the enemy and people because they deliver God's word. The devil hates prophets because they are God's mouthpiece.

A mouthpiece is:

- Someone who speaks for another person or for a group or organization.
- A spokesperson who speaks as the representative of another person.
- A person who expresses another person's wishes

The prophet speaks for God. He is God's representative on the earth and expresses the thoughts and desires of the Lord. The words that the prophet speaks is often one of correction. Because some people hate correction, they despise the prophet who is merely the messenger of God. In addition to prophesying the word of the Lord, prophets also anoint, release and ordain ministers.

The office of the prophet is distinct from someone who has the gift of prophecy . The prophet along with all the other five-fold ministers is a gift to the body of Christ. Someone with the gift of prophecy is not part of the five-fold ministry. They do not walk in the office of the prophet. They are <u>not</u> a gift to the body of Christ but <u>have</u> a gift-the gift of prophecy.

Prophecies are usually words of edification, exhortation, comfort, encouragement, direction, instruction, correction, judgment and warning. The prophet ministers all these, but more so correction, judgment and warning. Someone with a gift of prophecy very rarely prophesies correction, judgment and warning, and mostly prophesies edification, exhortation, comfort, encouragement, direction and instruction. A person who is not a prophet or does not have the gift of prophecy can also prophesy as the Holy Spirit moves upon them. This is called the Spirit of prophecy.

The Spirit of God can breathe upon anyone and cause him to prophesy. In addition, when someone is in the presence of a prophet who has a strong prophetic anointing, the Spirit of God can move on that person and cause him or her to prophesy. Biblical examples of this can be found in the following scripture verses.

Numbers 11: 16 – 25

[16] So the Lord said to Moses: "Gather to Me seventy men of the elders of Israel, whom you know to be the elders of the people and officers over them; bring them to the tabernacle of meeting, that they may stand there with you. [17] Then I will come down and talk with you there. I will take of the Spirit that *is* upon you and will put *the same* upon them; and they shall bear the burden of the people with you, that you may not bear *it* yourself alone. [18] Then you shall say to the people, 'Consecrate yourselves for tomorrow, and you shall eat meat; for you have wept in the hearing of the Lord, saying, "Who will give us meat to eat? For *it was* well with us in Egypt." Therefore the Lord will give you meat, and you shall eat. [19] You shall eat, not one day, nor two days, nor five days, nor ten days, nor twenty days, [20] but *for* a whole month, until it comes out of your nostrils and becomes loathsome to you, because you have despised the Lord who is among you, and have wept before Him, saying, "Why did we ever come up out of Egypt?" [21] And Moses said, "The people whom I *am* among *are* six hundred thousand men on foot; yet You have said, 'I will give them meat, that they may eat *for* a whole month.' [22] Shall flocks and herds be slaughtered for them, to provide enough for them? Or shall all the fish of the sea be gathered together for them, to provide enough for them?"

²³ And the Lord said to Moses, "Has the Lord's arm been shortened? Now you shall see whether what I say will happen to you or not." ²⁴ So Moses went out and told the people the words of the Lord, and he gathered the seventy men of the elders of the people and placed them around the tabernacle. ²⁵ Then the Lord came down in the cloud, and spoke to him, and took of the Spirit that *was* upon him, and placed *the same* upon the seventy elders; and it happened, when the Spirit rested upon them, that they prophesied, **although they never did *so* again.**

1 Sam 10: 1-6
¹Then Samuel took a flask of oil and poured *it* on his head, and kissed him and said: "*Is it* not because the Lord has anointed you commander over His inheritance? ² When you have departed from me today, you will find two men by Rachel's tomb in the territory of Benjamin at Zelzah; and they will say to you, 'The donkeys which you went to look for have been found. And now your father has ceased caring about the donkeys and is worrying about you, saying, "What shall I do about my son?" ' ³ Then you shall go on forward from there and come to the terebinth tree of Tabor. There three men going up to God at Bethel will meet you, one carrying three young goats, another carrying three loaves of bread, and another carrying a skin of wine. ⁴ And they will greet you and give you two *loaves* of bread, which you shall receive from their hands. ⁵ After that you shall come to the hill of God where the Philistine garrison *is*. And it will happen, when you have come there to the city, that you will meet a group of prophets coming down from the high place with a stringed instrument, a tambourine, a flute, and a harp before

them; and they will be prophesying. ⁶Then the Spirit of the Lord will come upon you, and you will prophesy with them and be turned into another man.

1 Sam 10: 9-11

⁹ So it was, when he had turned his back to go from Samuel, that God [gave him another heart; and all those signs came to pass that day. ¹⁰ When they came there to the hill, there was a group of prophets to meet him; then the Spirit of God came upon him, and he prophesied among them. ¹¹ And it happened, when all who knew him formerly saw that he indeed prophesied among the prophets, that the people said to one another, "**What *is* this *that* has come upon the son of Kish?** *Is* **Saul also among the prophets?**"

1 Sam. 19: 20-24

²⁰ Then Saul sent messengers to take David. And when they saw the group of prophets prophesying, and Samuel standing *as* leader over them, the Spirit of God came upon the messengers of Saul, **and they also prophesied.** ²¹ And when Saul was told, he sent other messengers, **and they prophesied likewise.** Then Saul sent messengers again the third time, **and they prophesied also.** ²² Then he also went to Ramah, and came to the great well that *is* at Sechu. So he asked, and said, "Where *are* Samuel and David?" And *someone* said, "Indeed *they* *are* at Naioth in Ramah." ²³ So he went there to Naioth in Ramah.

Then the Spirit of God was upon him also, and he went on and prophesied until he came to Naioth in Ramah. ²⁴ And he also stripped off his clothes and prophesied before Samuel in like manner, and lay down naked all that day and all that night. Therefore they say, "*Is* **Saul also among the prophets?**"

Unlike someone who prophesies when the Spirit of the Lord moves upon them to prophesy, the prophet can prophesy "at the drop of a hat". The phrase "at the drop of a hat" means quickly and without hesitation. The prophet must quickly and unhesitatingly prophesy the word of the Lord. The prophet continuously walks in the prophetic and does not have to "put it on".

Questions:

What is the difference between the Office of the prophet, the gift of prophecy and the Spirit of prophecy?

Which of the following scripture verses describes the Office of the prophet? Explain why: **Eph. 4: 11-16. Numbers 11: 16 – 25. 1 Sam 10: 1-6. 1 Sam 10: 9-11. 1 Sam. 19: 20-24**

Which of the following scripture verses describes the Spirit of prophecy? Explain why: **Eph. 4: 11-16. Numbers 11: 16 – 25. 1 Sam 10: 1-6. 1 Sam 10: 9-11. 1 Sam. 19: 20-24**

_____
_____
_____
_____
_____
_____
_____
_____
_____
_____
_____
_____
_____
_____
_____
_____
_____
_____
_____
_____
_____
_____

Chapter 2
What is Prophecy?

Prophecy is not divine revelation. Prophecy is the expression of the divine revelation given to the prophet by the Lord. That expression is then communicated by the prophet through prophetic utterances (spoken words, written words and songs). Three Hebrew words for prophecy are:

Nbuw'ah (*pronounced neb-oo-aw'*) a prediction (spoken or written).

5012 naba' (*pronounced naw-baw'*) to speak (or sing) by inspiration (in prediction)

Massa (*pronounced mas-saw*) an utterance; a song ; a burden. (Strong's Concordance with Hebrew and Greek Lexicon, 2021)

One of the Greek words for prophecy is propheteuo (prof-ate-yoo'-o), which means to foretell events, to speak under divine inspiration, and to exercise the prophetic office. (Strong's Concordance with Hebrew and Greek Lexicon, 2021).

Prophecy, therefore, is a spoken, sung or written prediction which is inspired by God and uttered through the prophet. The prophet uses speech, song and the written word to (1) reveal what is on God's heart and (2) express the thoughts and desires of the Lord.

Prophecies are usually words of edification, exhortation, comfort, direction, instruction, correction, judgment and warning. God uses the prophet to prophesy in this manner, but also uses apostles and prophets to prophesy words of edification, exhortation, comfort, direction, instruction, correction, judgment and warning to the prophet. The prophet is not exempt from instruction, correction, judgment and warning.

Edification
The Greek word used for "edification" in the New Testament is *oikodomé*, which means "the building of a house." The word *edify* is "to instruct and improve, especially in moral and religious knowledge." According to *Vine's Expository Dictionary of Old and New Testament Words*, the word edify means the spiritual building up and development of believers through prophecy and teaching (Vine's Expository Dictionary of New Testament Words, 2021).

Exhortation
The word exhort means to communicate to earnestly and emphatically urge someone to do something. Prophecies of exhortation are those that beseech and admonish a person to pursue a specific course of conduct.

Comfort
The word comfort means to relieve someone's sadness or sorrow. Prophecies of comfort soothe, console and encourage people who are sad and experiencing deep grief. Such prophecies provide the person with solace (comfort and consolation in a time of distress or sadness).

Direction

The word direction means the specified path that someone should take to reach a specific place or achieve a certain goal. Prophecies of direction reveal to people the way they should go or proceed in matters such as marriage, ministry, business, education, careers and relocation. The following scripture is an example of a prophecy of direction.

1 Samuel 9: 3-6, 10-20.
[3] Now the donkeys of Kish, Saul's father, were lost. And Kish said to his son Saul, "Please take one of the servants with you, and arise, go and look for the donkeys." [4] So he passed through the mountains of Ephraim and through the land of Shalisha, but they did not find *them*. Then they passed through the land of Shaalim, and *they were* not *there*. Then he passed through the land of the Benjamites, but they did not find *them*. [5] When they had come to the land of Zuph, Saul said to his servant who *was* with him, "Come, let us return, lest my father cease *caring* about the donkeys and become worried about us." [6] And he said to him, "Look now, *there is* in this city a man of God, and *he is* an honorable man; all that he says surely comes to pass. So let us go there; perhaps he can show us the way that we should go." [10] Then Saul said to his servant, "Well said; come, let us go." So they went to the city where the man of God *was*.
[11] As they went up the hill to the city, they met some young women going out to draw water, and said to them,
"Is the seer here?"[12] And they answered them and said, "Yes, there he is, just ahead of you. Hurry now; for today he came to this city, because there is a sacrifice of the people today on the high place. [14] So they went up to the city. As they were coming into the city, there was Samuel, coming out toward them on his way up to the high place.[15] Now

the Lord had told Samuel in his ear the day before Saul came, saying, [16] "Tomorrow about this time I will send you a man from the land of Benjamin, and you shall anoint him commander over My people Israel, that he may save My people from the hand of the Philistines; for I have looked upon My people, because their cry has come to Me."[17] So when Samuel saw Saul, the Lord said to him, "There he is, the man of whom I spoke to you. This one shall reign over My people." [18] Then Saul drew near to Samuel in the gate, and said, "Please tell me, where *is* the seer's house?" [19] Samuel answered Saul and said, "I *am* the seer. Go up before me to the high place, for you shall eat with me today; and tomorrow I will let you go and will tell you all that *is* in your heart. [20] But as for your donkeys that were lost three days ago, do not be anxious about them, for they have been found.

1 Samuel 10:1-6

[1] Then Samuel took a flask of oil and poured *it* on his head, and kissed him and said: "*Is it* not because the Lord has anointed you commander over His inheritance? [2] When you have departed from me today, you will find two men by Rachel's tomb in the territory of Benjamin at Zelzah; and they will say to you, 'The donkeys which you went to look for have been found. And now your father has ceased caring about the donkeys and is worrying about you, saying, "What shall I do about my son?" ' [3] Then you shall go on forward from there and come to the terebinth tree of Tabor. There three men going up to God at Bethel will meet you, one carrying three young goats, another carrying three loaves of bread, and another carrying a skin of wine. [4] And they will greet you and give you two *loaves* of bread,

which you shall receive from their hands. ⁵ After that you shall come to the hill of God where the Philistine garrison *is*. And it will happen, when you have come there to the city, that you will meet a group of prophets coming down from the high place with a stringed instrument, a tambourine, a flute, and a harp before them; and they will be prophesying. ⁶ Then the Spirit of the Lord will come upon you, and you will prophesy with them and be turned into another man.

Instruction

The word instruct means to tell or order someone to do something, especially in a formal or official way. Prophecies of instruction are meant to guide, teach and counsel someone in order for them to learn how to conduct themselves in specific situations. They are also meant to alter the person's course when they have gone astray.

Proverbs 15:32
³² He who despises instruction despises his own soul, But he who heeds rebuke gets understanding.

Psalm 32:8-10
⁸ I will instruct you and teach you in the way you should go; I will guide you with My eye. ⁹ Do not be like the horse *or* like the mule, *Which* have no understanding, Which must be harnessed with bit and bridle, Else they will not come near you.

Warning

The word warn means to admonish i.e. warn or reprimand someone firmly.

Jonah 3

¹ Now the word of the Lord came to Jonah the second time, saying, ² "Arise, go to Nineveh, that great city, and preach to it the message that I tell you." ³ So Jonah arose and went to Nineveh, according to the word of the Lord. Now Nineveh was an exceedingly great city, a three-day journey *in extent.* ⁴ And Jonah began to enter the city on the first day's walk. Then he cried out and said, "Yet forty days, and Nineveh shall be overthrown!" ⁵ So the people of Nineveh believed God, proclaimed a fast, and put on sackcloth, from the greatest to the least of them. ⁶ Then word came to the king of Nineveh; and he arose from his throne and laid aside his robe, covered *himself* with sackcloth and sat in ashes. ⁷ And he caused *it* to be proclaimed and published throughout Nineveh by the decree of the king and his nobles, saying, Let neither man nor beast, herd nor flock, taste anything; do not let them eat, or drink water. ⁸ But let man and beast be covered with sackcloth, and cry mightily to God; yes, let everyone turn from his evil way and from the violence that is in his hands. ⁹ Who can tell *if* God will turn and relent, and turn away from His fierce anger, so that we may not perish? ¹⁰ Then God saw their works, that they turned from their evil way; and God relented from the disaster that He had said He would bring upon them, and He did not do it.

Correction

The word correction means chastisement. To chastise someone is to make them understand that they have failed or done something wrong. God chastises people so that they can change or improve their behavior. God chastises the heathen, but also chastises those that are His sons and daughters.

Hebrews 12:6-11

⁶For whom the Lord loves He chastens, And scourges every son whom He receives. ⁷ If¹ you endure chastening, God deals with you as with sons; for what son is there whom a father does not chasten? ⁸ But if you are without chastening, of which all have become partakers, then you are illegitimate and not sons. ⁹ Furthermore, we have had human fathers who corrected *us,* and we paid *them* respect. Shall we not much more readily be in subjection to the Father of spirits and live? ¹⁰ For they indeed for a few days chastened *us* as seemed *best* to them, but for *our* profit, that *we* may be partakers of His holiness. ¹¹ Now no chastening seems to be joyful for the present, but painful; nevertheless, afterward it yields the peaceable fruit of righteousness to those who have been trained by it.

God uses Nathan, the prophet to correct David.

2 Sam. 12: 1-9

1 Then the Lord sent Nathan to David. And he came to him, and said to him: "There were two men in one city, one rich and the other poor. 2 The rich man had exceedingly many flocks and herds. 3 But the poor man had nothing, except one little ewe lamb which he had bought and nourished; and it grew up together with him and with his children. It ate of his own food and drank from his own cup and lay in his bosom; and it was like a daughter to him. ⁴ And a traveler came to the rich man, who refused to take from his own flock and from his own herd to prepare one for the wayfaring man who had come to him; but he took the poor man's lamb and prepared it for the man who had come to him."⁵ So David's anger was greatly aroused against the man, and he said to Nathan, "As the Lord lives, the man who has done this

[a]shall surely die! ⁶ And he shall restore fourfold for the lamb, because he did this thing and because he had no pity." ⁷ Then Nathan said to David, "You are the man! Thus says the Lord God of Israel: 'I anointed you king over Israel, and I delivered you from the hand of Saul. ⁸ I gave you your master's house and your master's wives into your keeping, and gave you the house of Israel and Judah. And if that had been too little, I also would have given you much more! ⁹ Why have you despised the commandment of the Lord, to do evil in His sight? You have killed Uriah the Hittite with the sword; you have taken his wife to be your wife, and have killed him with the sword of the people of Ammon.

Judgment
Before God releases his judgment, he first releases instruction, warning and then correction. When the person or nation does not obey God's instructions, he then releases a warning. If they do not heed his instruction, he then releases warning. If they do not heed his warning, he then releases correction. If they do not heed his correction, he then releases His judgment. These steps are usually released through the prophets. The prophet is also not exempt from receiving the instruction, warning, correction and judgment of the Lord. In 2 Sam. 12: 1-9, God used the prophet Nathan to correct David for his adulterous affair with Bathsheba and killing her husband, Uriah the Hittite. In the following verses, he uses Nathan to prophesy judgment to David.

2 Sam. 12: 10-12
¹⁰ Now therefore, the sword shall never depart from your house, because you have despised Me, and have taken the wife of Uriah the Hittite to be your wife.' ¹¹ Thus says the Lord: 'Behold, I will raise up adversity against you from

your own house; and I will take your wives before your eyes and give *them* to your neighbor, and he shall lie with your wives in the sight of this sun. ¹² For you did *it* secretly, but I will do this thing before all Israel, before the sun.'

Questions:
What is prophecy?
_____
_____
_____
_____
_____
_____
_____

Using the above teaching on the type of prophecies, please list scriptural examples of prophecies of edification, exhortation, comfort, direction, instruction, correction, judgment and warning. If you are unable to find any scriptures regarding these types of prophecies, please use examples of real prophecies you or others you know who have received these types of prophecies.

_____
_____
_____
_____

Chapter 3
Prophecy is important to God

Prophecy is extremely important to God for several reasons. God has a multitude of thoughts towards every person, and one of the ways he wants to express those thoughts to them is by using his prophets to do so.

> **Psalm 139:16-18**
> [16] Your eyes saw my substance, being yet unformed. And in Your book they all were written, The days fashioned for me, When *as yet there were* none of them. [17] How precious also are Your thoughts to me, O God! How great is the sum of them. [18] *If* I should count them, they would be more in number than the sand.

The Lord wants to communicate his heart to **all** people, whether they are saved or unsaved. There are prophetic words that the Lord has for the unsaved to draw them to Him – to bring about their salvation. One of the ways God communicates His heart (his feelings and his emotions) is through the prophet. Some of God's emotions are *joy, sorrow, anger and love*. People want to know how they Lord feels about them. Born again Christians need to know God's will for their lives. They need to know what ministry they are called to do. They need to know what direction they should go. They need words of comfort and encouragement. They may not receive revelation from the Lord or are unable to discern whether the revelation they do get is from Him . They may need confirmation on something that the Lord has revealed to them. Prophecies given to people are called personal prophecies. God also uses the prophet to release corporate prophecies to churches, groups, presidents, monarchs, a nation, nations and other organizations.

For these reasons, the prophetic word must always be accurate. False prophecies can derail a person's life. They can obstruct God's will for the person's life by diverting them from their intended course. False prophecies can alter the course of a nation. False prophecies can cause someone to marry the wrong person. False prophecies can cause presidents and other heads of state to make wrong decisions regarding the future of their country. The prophet should not add to or take away from the word that the Lord gives him to release.

The prophet must have strong discernment and exercise that discernment at all times. Discernment is the divine ability to identify what spirit is in operation through something or someone. There are three categories of spirits that we interact with daily. These are demonic spirits, human spirits (the flesh) and the Holy Spirit. These interactions come through conversations, dreams, visions and other channels. The devil and his evil horde of demonic spirits impart false revelation in order to deceive the prophet and other Christians. The prophet must have discernment so that he is nor deceived by fake revelation so that false prophecies will not be released. Discernment is a spiritual gift, but you may also ask the Lord for discernment.

Proverbs 2:3-4

³ Yes, if you cry out for discernment, *And* lift up your voice for understanding, ⁴ If you seek her as silver, And search for her as *for* hidden treasures; ⁵ Then you will understand the fear of the Lord, And find the knowledge of God.

With discernment, the prophet can go into any environment and quickly tell the spiritual atmosphere of the people and the place. With discernment, the prophet can go into any environment and tell what spirits are in operation. With discernment, the prophet can sense what spirit is influencing a person. With discernment, the prophet can distinguish truth from error. With discernment, the prophet can discern whether someone is operating in the Spirit or in the flesh.

Questions:
Why is prophecy important to God?

_____
_____
_____
_____
_____
_____
_____
_____
_____
_____

Chapter 4
God, the Revealer:
The Prophet, the Revelator

God is the revealer and the prophet is the revelator. To reveal something to someone, means that the thing being revealed is hidden. A revealer, therefore, is a person who reveals what is hidden. God the revealer, reveals things to the prophet that cannot be seen, heard or sensed by natural means. The prophet is the revelator, one that reveals the heart and will of God. In order for the prophet to reveal the heart and will of God, he must first receive revelation from the Lord. When prophets get revelation from the Lord, they often confuse what the get as being something that will happen in the future. The revelation from the Lord reveals the past, the present and the future.

Revelation is downloaded to the prophet by the Lord in any of the following and varied ways: the still small voice of the Lord; the audible voice of the Lord; dreams; visions; still images ; impressions and trances.

> **Hebrews 1:1**.
> God, who at various times and in various ways spoke in time past to the fathers by the prophets.

Download is defined as "to copy or transfer data into the memory of one computer system from a larger one" (Dictionary.com, 2013). Data is stored information.

God transfers divine revelation from His infinite (limitless, impossible to measure or calculate) and vast being into the memory of his prophets who are finite (limited in size and extent) and who "see through a glass darkly". To "see through a glass darkly" refers to the prophet's obscured and imperfect vision. The prophet cannot see or know anything using his natural senses, nor can he see and know all things in the spirit. The prophet only sees and knows what the Lord reveals to him. The Apostle Paul, under the inspiration of the Holy Spirit, in his letter to the Corinthians expressed this.

1 Corinthians 13:12
[12] For now we see in a mirror, dimly, but then face to face. Now I know in part, but then I shall know just as I also am known.

The Amplified Version of the Bible explains this even further.

1 Corinthians 13:12
Amplified Bible
[12] For now [in this time of imperfection] we see in a mirror dimly [a blurred reflection, a riddle, an enigma], but then [when the time of perfection comes we will see reality] face to face. Now I know in part [just in fragments], but then I will know fully, just as I have been fully known [by God].

The Apostle Paul, who had an open visitation from the Lord on the Damascus Road and heard the voice of God and experienced visions on so many other occasions was explaining that his revelation of the things of God was limited, like seeing through a "mirror dimly [a blurred reflection, a riddle, an enigma]".

How God downloads revelation to the prophet.

You must first have an understanding of the earthly realm and the spiritual realm in order to understand how God downloads revelation to the prophet. A realm is defined as "the region, sphere, or domain within which anything occurs, prevails, or dominates, a kingdom" (Dictionary.com, 2013). There are two major realms: the earthly realm and the spiritual realm. The earthly realm, which is the world, is visible. In the earthly realm we use our earthly senses –hearing, touch, sight, smell and taste. Our earthly senses respond tangibly *(capable of being touched; discernible by the touch; material or substantial* (Dictionary.com, 2013)*)* to everything in the earthly realm (except in cases where a person has lost one, some or all of their earthly senses) . The spiritual realm is invisible and is all around us, yet we cannot see it or experience except by revelation from God. Just as we have earthly senses, so too do we have spiritual senses. However, our spiritual senses do not respond as do our earthly senses. Our spiritual senses have to be developed.

God reveals things that are hidden to our earthly senses (hearing, touching, seeing, smelling and tasting) using the spiritual senses (seeing, hearing, touching, smelling and tasting). That revelation is divinely breathed in by the Holy Spirit. It is a partnership between the Holy Spirit and the prophet's human spirit.

Hearing

The Lord downloads revelation by speaking to the prophet. The prophet must be able to hear and know the voice of the Lord. In the earthly realm, a person cannot hear properly when there is noise.

When there is spiritual noise, the prophet cannot hear the voice of the Lord. Spiritual noise is distractions, disturbances, attitudes, perceptions, mindsets, strongholds, and sin. Your spiritual ears must be open and acute in order to hear and know the voice of the Lord. God's voice can be heard internally or externally.

Internally
The Lord speaks in a still, small voice that is heard internally. You hear His voice on the inside of you-in your entire being. His voice is so still (quiet) and small (slight) that it can be indiscernible (not clearly distinguished) and may go undetected.

Externally
The audible voice of the Lord is heard externally. You hear it on the outside of your being, just as you would hear someone speaking to you. The prophet Samuel, as a young boy, initially did not know the voice of the Lord. When the Lord first spoke to him, he thought it was Eli the priest that was speaking.

1 Samuel 3
Now the boy Samuel ministered to the Lord before Eli. And the word of the Lord was rare in those days; *there was* no widespread revelation. ² And it came to pass at that time, while Eli *was* lying down in his place, and when his eyes had begun to grow so dim that he could not see, ³ and before the lamp of God went out in the tabernacle of the Lord where the ark of God *was,* and while Samuel was lying down, ⁴ that the Lord called Samuel. And he answered, "Here

I am!" ⁵ So he ran to Eli and said, "Here I am, for you called me." And he said, "I did not call; lie down again." And he went and lay down. ⁶ Then the Lord called yet again, "Samuel!" So Samuel arose and went to Eli, and said, "Here I am, for you called me." He answered, "I did not call, my son; lie down again." ⁷ (Now Samuel did not yet know the Lord, nor was the word of the Lord yet revealed to him.) ⁸ And the Lord called Samuel again the third time. So he arose and went to Eli, and said, "Here I am, for you did call me. "Then Eli perceived that the Lord had called the boy. ⁹ Therefore Eli said to Samuel, "Go, lie down; and it shall be, if He calls you, that you must say, 'Speak, Lord, for Your servant hears.' " So Samuel went and lay down in his place. ¹⁰ Now the Lord came and stood and called as at other times, "Samuel! Samuel!"

And Samuel answered, "Speak, for Your servant hears." ¹¹ Then the Lord said to Samuel: "Behold, I will do something in Israel at which both ears of everyone who hears it will tingle. ¹² In that day I will perform against Eli all that I have spoken concerning his house, from beginning to end. ¹³ For I have told him that I will judge his house forever for the iniquity which he knows, because his sons made themselves vile, and he did not ʲrestrain them. ¹⁴ And therefore I have sworn to the house of Eli that the iniquity of Eli's house shall not be atoned for by sacrifice or offering forever." ¹⁵ So Samuel lay down until ˡmorning, and opened the doors of the house of the Lord. And Samuel was afraid to tell Eli the vision. ¹⁶ Then Eli called Samuel and said, "Samuel, my son! "He answered, "Here I am." ¹⁷ And he said, "What *is* the word that *the Lord* spoke to you? Please do not hide *it* from me. God do so to you, and more also, if you hide anything from me of all the things that He said to you." ¹⁸ Then Samuel told him everything, and hid nothing from him. And he said, "It *is* the Lord. Let Him do what seems good to Him." ¹⁹ So Samuel grew, and the Lord was with him and let none of his words fall to the ground. ²⁰ And all Israel from Dan to Beersheba knew that Samuel *had been* established as a prophet of the Lord. ²¹ Then the Lord appeared again in Shiloh. For the Lord revealed Himself to Samuel in Shiloh by the word of the Lord.

Here are some other instances recorded in the Bible when the Lord spoke to people in an audible voice.

Acts 9: 1-7
¹Then Saul, still breathing threats and murder against the disciples of the Lord, went to the high priest ² and

asked letters from him to the synagogues of Damascus, so that if he found any who were of the Way, whether men or women, he might bring them bound to Jerusalem. ³ As he journeyed he came near Damascus, and suddenly a light shone around him from heaven. ⁴ Then he fell to the ground, and heard a voice saying to him, "Saul, Saul, why are you persecuting Me?" ⁵ And he said, "Who are You, Lord?"
Then the Lord said, "I am Jesus, whom you are persecuting. It *is* hard for you to kick against the goads."⁶ So he, trembling and astonished, said, "Lord, what do You want me to do?" Then the Lord *said* to him, "Arise and go into the city, and you will be told what you must do." ⁷ And the men who journeyed with him stood speechless, hearing a voice but seeing no one.

Matt 3: 16-17
¹⁶ When He had been baptized, Jesus came up immediately from the water; and behold, the heavens were opened to Him, and He saw the Spirit of God descending like a dove and alighting upon Him. ¹⁷ And suddenly a voice came from heaven, saying, "This is My beloved Son, in whom I am well pleased."

John 12: 27-30
²⁷ "Now My soul is troubled, and what shall I say? 'Father, save Me from this hour'? But for this purpose I came to this hour. ²⁸ Father, glorify Your name." Then a voice came from heaven, *saying,* "I have both glorified *it* and will glorify *it* again."²⁹ Therefore the people who stood by and heard *it* said that it had thundered. Others said, "An angel has spoken to Him."³⁰ Jesus answered and said, "This voice did not come because of Me, but for your sake.

Touching

One of the Hebrew words for touch is muwsh *(pronounced moosh)* which means to feel. God reveals things to the prophet through a "feeling". The prophet feels or senses the revelation from the Lord using his spiritual senses. This is called and impression. An impression is a deep knowing within the prophet's spirit of the revelation that the Lord has downloaded to the prophet. An impression is revelation from God that is communicated to the prophet **not** by hearing or seeing but by a deep knowing inside the prophet. The word impress means: (a) to apply with pressure so as to imprint; (b) to produce (as a mark) by pressure (c) to mark by or as if by pressure or stamping (Dictionary.com, 2013). An impression from the Lord is an imprint (to fix indelibly or permanently as on the memory) in your spirit that produces pressure (the application of force to something by something else in direct contact with it) within the Prophet and a deep knowing inside the prophet that "you know that you know that you know".

Seeing

Seeing is in the domain of the seer prophet. The Seer prophet is a type of prophet who sees through his spiritual eyes. The word seer means a beholder in vision. The seer sees visions, dreams and images and goes into trances. The "seer" beholds the vision of God, and prophesies according to what he sees in the Spirit.

Dreams

A dream is a sequence of moving images in which the prophet may experience seeing, hearing, touching, smelling, tasting and emotions while asleep. Dreams can come from a human spirit (you), a demonic spirit or the Holy Spirit.

Dreams from you
Dreams can come from you.

> **Jeremiah 29: 8**
> For thus says the Lord of hosts, the God of Israel: Do not let your prophets and your diviners who are in your midst deceive you, nor listen to your dreams which you cause to be dreamed.

Dreams that come from you result from acting out unfilled emotions and expectations that were not acted out during the day. **Ecclesiastes 5:3** -*For a **dream** comes through much activity*. Whenever you suppress your feelings and experiences you have, they may very likely be expressed in your dreams. For example, if you were angry with someone and suppressed that anger, you may express that unfulfilled anger in your dreams. Traumatic experiences may also affect the content of your dreams. Dreams from you, therefore, are those where you are acting out experiences and situations that you have not been able to do during the day. Examples of this are unfulfilled desires, careers and marriages. Dreams from you can also be recurring dreams in which you are enacting out an unfulfilled desire.

Dreams from the enemy
The devil is an angel of light who counterfeits everything possible in the Kingdom of God.

> **2 Cor. 11:14**
> For Satan himself transforms himself into an angel of light.

Dreams from the enemy are false dreams which are meant to deceive the prophet. The enemy's dreams are often half-truths and half- lies. Dreams from the Lord are complete truths. The enemy mixes truth and error so as to deceive the prophet into believing that the dream came from the Lord.

Dreams from the enemy reveal Satan's plans. They are meant to terrorize the dreamer. If the enemy cannot harass you when you are awake, he will do it when you are sleeping – to bring fear, torment, confusion and false direction. Dreams from the enemy are to counterfeit any plan of God concerning you. Reject and cancel all dreams that come from the enemy immediately!

Dreams from the Lord

As previously stated - a dream is a sequence of moving images in which the prophet may experience seeing, hearing, touching, smelling, tasting and emotions while asleep. Dreams that come from the Lord contain all these elements. All your senses are heightened. Everything in the dream is vivid and magnified. Dreams from the Lord can be symbolic or literal.

Symbolic Dreams

The word symbolic means "representing something else". Symbolic dreams are loaded with symbols.

A symbol can be a person, a sign, a shape, a word or an object that is used to represent something else. Symbolic dreams cannot be taken literally. Symbolic dreams are usually vivid, extremely colorful, exaggerated and dramatic. They overemphasize issues and situations to get you to take notice of the dream and take action. Symbolic dreams stay on your mind when you are awake.

Dream Interpretation

Symbolic dreams are "dark sayings" that require interpretation. The interpretation of dreams is a gift from the Lord.

> **Numbers 12: 6-8**
> Then He said,
> "Hear now My words:
> If there is a prophet among you,
> *I*, the Lord, make Myself known to him in a vision;
> I speak to him in a dream.
> [7] Not so with My servant Moses;
> He *is* faithful in all My house.
> [8] I speak with him face to face,
> Even plainly, and not in dark sayings;
>
> **Job 33: 14-15**
> For God may speak in one way, or in another,
> *Yet man* does not perceive it.
> [15] In a dream, in a vision of the night,
> When deep sleep falls upon men,
> While slumbering on their beds.

God sometimes communicates in dark sayings for 2 reasons:
    (1) to hide the revelation from the enemy
    (2) To propel the prophet to go deeper in the things of God.

You have to seek the Lord for the meaning of the symbolic dream. To interpret a dream, you have to consider the entire dream, not just the symbolism. Ask the Lord for the interpretation of the dream! The prophet Daniel asked for the interpretation (**Daniel 2**).

First, identify the source of the dream using divine discernment. Is the dream from you, the enemy or God? Dreams from the Lord are vibrant, dramatic, and significant, colorful and detailed. You can see details. You can "feel the wind and the sun" so to speak. All your senses at intensified. Everything in the dream is significant. Do not leave out any of the elements in the dream. Remember that everything in a dream from the Lord has meaning.

Always record your dreams. Record your dream as soon as you awake. Ask, and write down, the answers to the following questions regarding the dream. If you have the gift of dream interpretation, ask the person who needs their dream interpreted the following questions as well.

- Is the dream black, white, gray or colorful?
- Who is doing what?
- Who is speaking?
- Who is in control?
- What is happening in the dream?
- When is it happening?
- Where is the dream taking place
- What are **all** the elements in the dream?
- How is the dream unfolding?
- What is the dream speaking of – life, death, health, destruction, prosperity, poverty etc.?
- Does the dream encourage or discourage you?
- Does the dream oppress or torment you?
- Does it motivate you into action?
- What is the conclusion of the dream or vision?
- How do you feel when you emerge from the dream– dirty, perverted, evil, disgusted?

Literal Dreams

Literal dreams do not require an interpretation. It is what it is. Here are some biblical examples of literal dreams.

1 Kings 3: 5-15

[5] At Gibeon the Lord appeared to Solomon in a dream by night; and God said, "Ask! What shall I give you?" [6] And Solomon said: "You have shown great mercy to Your servant David my father, because he walked before You in truth, in righteousness, and in uprightness of heart with You; You have continued this great kindness for him, and You have given him a son to sit on his throne, as *it is* this day. [7] Now, O Lord my God, You have made Your servant king instead of my father David, but I *am* a little child; I do not know *how* to go out or come in. [8] And Your servant *is* in the midst of Your people whom You have chosen, a great people, too numerous to be numbered or counted. [9] Therefore give to Your servant an understanding heart to judge Your people, that I may discern between good and evil. For who is able to judge this great people of Yours?" [10] The speech pleased the Lord, that Solomon had asked this thing. [11] Then God said to him:" Because you have asked this thing, and have not asked long life for yourself, nor have asked riches for yourself, nor have asked the life of your enemies, but have asked for yourself understanding to discern justice, [12] behold, I have done according to your words; see, I have given you a wise and understanding heart, so that there has not been anyone like you before you, nor shall any like you arise after you. [13] And I have also given you what you have not asked: both riches and honor, so that there shall not be anyone like you among the kings all your days. [14] So if you walk in My ways, to keep My statutes and My commandments, as your father David walked, then I will lengthen your days."

¹⁵ Then Solomon awoke; and indeed it had been a dream. And he came to Jerusalem and stood before the ark of the covenant of the Lord, offered up burnt offerings, offered peace offerings, and made a feast for all his servants.

Matthew 1: 18-20
¹⁸ Now the birth of Jesus Christ was as follows: After His mother Mary was betrothed to Joseph, before they came together, she was found with child of the Holy Spirit. ¹⁹ Then Joseph her husband, being a just *man,* and not wanting to make her a public example, was minded to put her away secretly. ²⁰ But while he thought about these things, behold, an angel of the Lord appeared to him in a dream, saying, "Joseph, son of David, do not be afraid to take to you Mary your wife, for that which is conceived in her is of the Holy Spirit.

Matthew 2: 12-13
¹² Then, being divinely warned in a dream that they should not return to Herod, they departed for their own country another way.
¹³ Now when they had departed, behold, an angel of the Lord appeared to Joseph in a dream, saying, "Arise, take the young Child and His mother, flee to Egypt, and stay there until I bring you word; for Herod will seek the young Child to destroy Him.

Matthew 27: 19
¹⁹ While he (Pilate) was sitting on the judgment seat, his wife sent to him, saying, "Have nothing to do with that just Man, for I have suffered many things today in a dream because of Him.

Visions

Visions like dreams are moving images, except that you are wide awake. A vision can occur at any time of the day (or night). Visions can be literal or symbolic.

Gen. 15: 1

¹ After these things the word of the Lord came to Abram in a vision, saying, "Do not be afraid, Abram.
I *am* your shield, your exceedingly great reward."

Matt. 17: 1-9

Now after six days Jesus took Peter, James, and John his brother, led them up on a high mountain by themselves; ² and He was transfigured before them. His face shone like the sun, and His clothes became as white as the light. ³ And behold, Moses and Elijah appeared to them, talking with Him. ⁴ Then Peter answered and said to Jesus, "Lord, it is good for us to be here; if You wish, let us make here three tabernacles: one for You, one for Moses, and one for Elijah." ⁵ While he was still speaking, behold, a bright cloud overshadowed them; and suddenly a voice came out of the cloud, saying, "This is My beloved Son, in whom I am well pleased. Hear Him!" ⁶ And when the disciples heard *it*, they fell on their faces and were greatly afraid. ⁷ But Jesus came and touched them and said, "Arise, and do not be afraid." ⁸ When they had lifted up their eyes, they saw no one but Jesus only. ⁹ Now as they came down from the mountain, Jesus commanded them, saying, "Tell the vision to no one until the Son of Man is risen from the dead."

Acts 7: 54-56
Stephen the Martyr
⁵⁴ When they heard these things they were [cut to the heart, and they gnashed at him with *their* teeth. ⁵⁵ But he, being full of the Holy Spirit, gazed into heaven and saw the glory of God, and Jesus standing at the right hand of God, ⁵⁶ and said, "Look! I see the heavens opened and the Son of Man standing at the right hand of God!"

Isaiah 6: 1-2
In the year that King Uzziah died, I saw the Lord sitting on a throne, high and lifted up, and the train of His *robe* filled the temple. ² Above it stood seraphim; each one had six wings: with two he covered his face, with two he covered his feet, and with two he flew.

Acts 9:10-12
¹⁰ Now there was a certain disciple at Damascus named Ananias; and to him the Lord said in a vision, "Ananias."
And he said, "Here I am, Lord."¹¹ So the Lord *said* to him, "Arise and go to the street called Straight, and inquire at the house of Judas for *one* called Saul of Tarsus, for behold, he is praying. ¹² And in a vision he has seen a man named Ananias coming in and putting *his* hand on him, so that he might receive his sight.

Also read Ezekiel 1 and Ezekiel 37

Questions:
Which of the scripture verses above are examples of literal and symbolic visions? Why?

_____

_____

_____

_____

_____

_____

_____

A vision can have sound or no sound.

Example of a vison without sound

Acts 7: 54-56
Stephen the Martyr
⁵⁴ When they heard these things they were [cut to the heart, and they gnashed at him with *their* teeth. ⁵⁵ But he, being full of the Holy Spirit, gazed into heaven and saw the glory of God, and Jesus standing at the right hand of God, ⁵⁶ and said, "Look! I see the heavens opened and the Son of Man standing at the right hand of God!"

Examples of A vision with sound

Ezekiel 37: 1-7
The hand of the Lord came upon me and brought me out in the Spirit of the Lord, and set me down in the midst of the valley; and it *was* full of bones. ² Then He caused me to pass by them all around, and behold, *there were* very many in the open valley; and indeed *they were* very dry. ³ And He said to me, "Son of man, can these bones live?" So I answered, "O Lord God, You know." ⁴ Again He said to me, "Prophesy to

these bones, and say to them, 'O dry bones, hear the word of the Lord! ⁵ Thus says the Lord God to these bones:

"Surely I will cause breath to enter into you, and you shall live. ⁶ I will put sinews on you and bring flesh upon you, cover you with skin and put breath in you; and you shall live. Then you shall know that I *am* the Lord." ' "⁷ So I prophesied as I was commanded; and as I prophesied, there was a noise, and suddenly a rattling; and the bones came together, bone to bone.

Types of Visions

Similitude Vision

The word similitude means (1) similar (2) something closely resembling another (Dictionary, 2013). God will use familiar things or persons in a vision, *or a dream*, to make you feel comfortable and help you understand what He is revealing. In a similitude vision, you will find elements like your mother, father, brother, church members, and the house you lived in as a child, but they may actually represent a type of relationship or a memorable experience you had.

Acts 16: 9-15

⁹ And a vision appeared to Paul in the night. A man of Macedonia stood and pleaded with him, saying, "Come over to Macedonia and help us." ¹⁰ Now after he had seen the vision, immediately we sought to go to Macedonia, concluding that the Lord had called us to preach the gospel to them.

Paul saw a man in his vision, but when he got to Macedonia it was a woman who actually asked him for help.

Acts 16: 13-15

¹³ And on the Sabbath day we went out of the city to the riverside, where prayer was customarily made; and we sat down and spoke to the women who met *there*. ¹⁴ Now a certain woman named Lydia heard *us*. She was a seller of purple from the city of Thyatira, who worshiped God. The Lord opened her heart to heed the things spoken by Paul. ¹⁵ And when she and her household were baptized, she begged *us*, saying, "If you have judged me to be faithful to the Lord, come to my house and stay." So she persuaded us.

Interactive Visions

An interactive vision is one where the Lord or angelic beings are conversing and interacting with the prophet in the vision, *or dream.*

Genesis 46:1-3

46 So Israel took his journey with all that he had, and came to Beersheba, and offered sacrifices to the God of his father Isaac. ² Then God spoke to Israel in the visions of the night, and said, "Jacob, Jacob!" And he said, "Here I am."
³ So He said, "I *am* God, the God of your father; do not fear to go down to Egypt, for I will make of you a great nation there.

Dream Vision

A dream vision is a dream with a vision in the dream. In the dream you are having a vision.

Inner Vision

An inner vision is seen inside you through the eyes of the spirit. In an inner vision, your role is passive. You are an observer. You are looking at the vision on the outside. It is like watching a movie on television.

Open Vision

An open vision is different from an inner vision. In an open vision, your role is participatory. You are not an observer. You have a dynamic role. You are not just being shown something. You actually become part of the vision and you interact with the objects and persons in it. It is as if you are thrust into the vision. It is like you are actually in a movie on television. In the most dramatic of open visions you can hear, see, taste, feel and smell the things that are happening around you.

Ezekiel 3: 12-15

[12] Then the Spirit lifted me up, and I heard behind me a great thunderous voice: "Blessed is the glory of the Lord from His place!" [13] I also heard the noise of the wings of the living creatures that touched one another, and the noise of the wheels beside them, and a great thunderous noise. [14] So the Spirit lifted me up and took me away, and I went in bitterness, in the [a]heat of my spirit; but the hand of the Lord was strong upon me. [15] Then I came to the captives at Tel Abib, who dwelt by the River Chebar; and I sat where they sat, and remained there astonished among them seven days.

Revelation 1: 9-20

[9] I, John, both your brother and companion in the tribulation and kingdom and patience of Jesus Christ, was on the island that is called Patmos for the word of God and for the testimony of Jesus Christ.

[10] I was in the Spirit on the Lord's Day, and I heard behind me a loud voice, as of a trumpet, [11] saying, "I am the Alpha and the Omega, the First and the Last," and, "What you see, write in a book and send *it* to the seven churches which are in Asia: to Ephesus, to Smyrna, to Pergamos, to Thyatira, to Sardis, to Philadelphia, and to Laodicea." [12] Then I turned to see the voice that spoke with me. And having turned I saw seven golden lampstands, [13] and in the midst of the seven lampstands *One* like the Son of Man, clothed with a garment down to the feet and girded about the chest with a golden band. [14] His head and hair *were* white like wool, as white as snow, and His eyes like a flame of fire; [15] His feet *were* like fine brass, as if refined in a furnace, and His voice as the sound of many waters; [16] He had in His right hand seven stars, out of His mouth went a sharp two-edged sword, and His countenance *was* like the sun shining in its strength. [17] And when I saw Him, I fell at His feet as dead. But He laid His right hand on me, saying to me, "Do not be afraid; I am the First and the Last. [18] I *am* He who lives, and was dead, and behold, I am alive forevermore. Amen. And I have the keys of Hades and of Death. [19] Write the things which you have seen, and the things which are, and the things which will take place after this. [20] The mystery of the seven stars which you saw in My right hand, and the seven golden lampstands: The seven stars are the angels of the seven churches, and the seven lampstands which you saw are the seven churches.

Trance

The Greek word for trance is ekstasis, from which the word "ecstasy" is derived. It denotes the state of one who is "out of himself". In a trance you are wide-awake and suddenly you are taken to another place.

A trance is when the Lord takes your spirit out of your body and takes you to somewhere to reveal something to you. You are actually in the vision but your body is still in the location you were at before the trance occurred. You become conscious that you are in two places at the same time.

Acts 10: 9-16
⁹ The next day, as they went on their journey and drew near the city, Peter went up on the housetop to pray, about [c]the sixth hour. ¹⁰ Then he became very hungry and wanted to eat; but while they made ready, he fell into a trance ¹¹ and saw heaven opened and an object like a great sheet bound at the four corners, descending to him and let down to the earth. ¹² In it were all kinds of four-footed animals of the earth, wild beasts, creeping things, and birds of the air. ¹³ And a voice came to him, "Rise, Peter; kill and eat." ¹⁴ But Peter said, "Not so, Lord! For I have never eaten anything common or unclean." ¹⁵ And a voice *spoke* to him again the second time, "What God has cleansed you must not call common." ¹⁶ This was done three times. And the object was taken up into heaven again.

Acts 22: 17-21
¹⁷ "Now it happened, when I returned to Jerusalem and was praying in the temple, that I was in a trance ¹⁸ and saw Him saying to me, 'Make haste and get out of Jerusalem quickly, for they will not receive your testimony concerning Me.' ¹⁹ So I said, 'Lord, they know that in every synagogue I imprisoned and beat those who believe on You. ²⁰ And when the blood of Your martyr Stephen was shed, I also was standing by consenting to his death, and guarding the clothes of those who were killing him.' ²¹ Then He said to me, 'Depart, for I will send you far from here to the Gentiles.' "

Still Images
Images are motionless pictures like photographs that flash in front of you. It is like a could be words or an actual picture.

Smelling
The Lord also downloads revelation to the prophet through the spiritual sense of smell. These odors are very distinctive, and each odor denotes a different meaning. Smells also stir up your emotions, bring back memories, and often remind you of pleasant and unpleasant events. A sweet smelling aroma is usually associated with the presence of the Lord and worship unto him.

Genesis 8:20-21
[20] And Noah built an altar to the Lord, and took of every [ceremonially] clean animal and of every clean bird and offered burnt offerings on the altar. [21] The Lord smelled the pleasing aroma [a soothing, satisfying scent] and the Lord said to Himself, "I will never again curse the ground because of man, for the intent (strong inclination, desire) of man's heart is wicked from his youth; and I will never again destroy every living thing, as I have done.

Exodus 29:17-19
[17] Then you shall cut the ram in pieces, wash its entrails and its legs, and put *them* with its pieces and with its head. [18] And you shall burn the whole ram on the altar. It *is* a burnt offering to the Lord; it *is* a sweet aroma, an offering made by fire to the Lord.

Leviticus 3: 5
[5] and Aaron's sons shall burn it on the altar upon the burnt sacrifice, which *is* on the wood that *is* on the fire, as an offering made by fire, a sweet aroma to the Lord.

Tasting

The Lord will also communicate to the prophet through taste. The prophet may experience a variety of tastes such as a sweet salty or bitter taste in his mouth which denotes different things the Lord wants to reveal to the prophet. This is not through actually tasting food, drink or other substances, but it is through the spiritual sense of taste.

The Nabiy Prophet

Nabiy *(pronounced nah bee)* literally means "to bubble up" or "bubble forth as from a fountain". The Nabiy prophet does not usually see or hear in the Spirit, the word just bubbles forth out of him. The prophecy springs forth out of the Nabiy prophet's mouth like a steady stream of flowing water.

Questions:

What is the difference between an inner vision and an open vision?

_____

_____

_____

_____

_____

_____

_____

What is the difference between an open vision and a trance?

What is a similitude vision?

Chapter 5
Prophetic Protocol

Protocol is:

- the official procedure or system of rules and acceptable behaviors governing affairs of state or diplomatic occasions
- the system of rules and acceptable behaviour used at official ceremonies and occasions.
- the rules of conduct and etiquette required by a group or organization.

In international politics, diplomatic protocol is the etiquette of diplomacy and affairs of state. Protocols differ in each nation. For example, when speaking to the president of the United States you do not call them by their first or last name. You address them by the title of "Mr." or "Madam" which shows your respect for the office of the president. When the president enters the room, everyone who is seated must rise as a sign of respect. The president will then indicate when those who have risen may take their seats.

Just as there are protocols in the earthly realm, so too are their protocols in the spiritual realm in which the Kingdom of Heaven exists, and there are prophetic protocols.
The prophet is expected to know and apply prophetic protocols at all times. Here are some of the major protocols that the prophet is required to follow.

Prophesying to Leaders
Be careful how and when you prophesy to leaders especially in the presence of their congregation and members. If the prophecy is very personal and sensitive, prophesy to the leader in privacy.

Prophesy with diplomacy and tact
Diplomacy and tact are skills that are based on understanding people and being sensitive to their feelings. How you deliver a word can make a difference to whether or not someone receives it. Your tone should reflect the heart of God, which is love. Delivering words of correction, judgment (not yours but God's) and warning must also be done with diplomacy and the heart of God- the character of God.

Do not prophesy in a spooky or religious tone
Prophesying in a spooky, religious or lofty tone can cause fear and unease. So does talking in ancient English. For example using "thee and thou". Be real. Use terms and phrases that can be understood by the recipients of the prophecy.

Apologize if the prophecy is false
A true and authentic prophet can deliver a false prophecy if the prophet has been deceived by the enemy or if the prophet prophesies out of his emotions. It does not mean that the prophet is a false prophet. The prophet should then tell the person that they made a mistake so that the person does not continue to believe a false prophecy. Admit if you are wrong. That is called prophetic integrity. A prophet who fails to do this is full of pride.

Releasing a "prophecy" if you don't have one
If you are not getting any revelation from the Lord for the person, persons. group, organization etc, it is okay to say that

you are not getting anything. However you should still pray for the person, as the Holy Spirit directs. Do not release a false prophecy just to look, feel and sound good, or to appease the person. It is better to say nothing rather than release a false prophecy that would derail the person's life. Be determined to be accurate....not because you just want to be accurate but because you do not want to derail the person's life,

Prophesy exactly what the Lord tells you to release.
Do not add to or take away from the prophecy. Do not interject your opinion in the prophecy. Do not say you did not get anything from God and then share your opinion or experience as though it was a prophecy. It must be **only** what the Lord has revealed. As a rule, leave your flesh out of the prophecy. It must be the Lord and the Lord **alone** is speaking to the person - through you of course.

Do not prophesy based on what you see, know and heard (in the natural))
Remove biases, preconceived ideas and information that you have about the person, place, situation, church, group etc. Do not judge the outward appearance. Use your spiritual senses, **not** your natural senses. Get rid of formulas and traditions.

Have a prophet or apostle that you are accountable to
Have an authentic, mature prophet or apostle that you are accountable to. Be humble and teachable. Receive correction so that you can develop your prophetic gifting.

Do not speak or pray when someone else is prophesying.
The person cannot hear if you speak, pray or make noise when another person is prophesying. Remember that it is the Lord speaking through the other prophet and if you speak, pray or

make noise when the prophecy is being released, you are interrupting God. Do not be moved by the body language/facial expression of the person/persons you are prophesying to.

Prophetic Plagiarism

Prophets who are ministering on a team, often get the same revelation for a person, place, organization, church or other entity. When the first prophet prophesies what you also got from the Lord, still prophesy it. But you should always confirm a prophecy given by someone else by prophesying it also but confirming what the other prophet/prophets said. Start the prophecy by saying "I confirm what prophet so and so said. I also got the same thing" **And you can then reiterate it!!** Do not claim a prophesy another prophet prophesied as your own. This is called prophetic plagiarism. Plagiarism is "presenting someone else's work or ideas as your own, with or without their consent, by incorporating it into your work without full acknowledgement" (Oxford Dictionary, 2021).

Ask the Lord if or when you should release revelation

Do not blurt out every revelation you get from the Lord. Prophesy must be released in God's timing or not at all if the Lord directs. Ask the Lord the following: Should it be prophesied? If it should be prophesied, when should it be prophesied? Should it be prophesied openly or privately? If prophesying to a leader in the presence of their members, will the prophecy force the leader to do something God did not tell them to do?

Questions:

What is prophetic protocol?

_____

_____

Chapter 6
Methods of Prophesying

Revelation from the Lord reveals the past, the present and the future. When prophets get revelation from the Lord, they often erroneously believe that the revelation is something that will happen in the future. The revelation from the Lord reveals the past, the present and the future. The revelation downloaded to the prophet is released through prophetic utterances (spoken words, written words and songs). Those prophetic utterance may be personal or corporate. Personal prophecy is prophecy to an individual that is personal in nature and meant only for that person. Most personal prophecy is conditional. Corporate prophecy is prophecy that is not personal in nature, but which is meant for a group of people collectively.

Revelation about the past and present
Past and present revelation are words of knowledge. A word of knowledge are certain facts, past or present, about a person people, place or season. A word of knowledge is based on divine revelation of the Holy Spirit and not on human knowledge or perception. It is not based on intuition or the person's body language. It is given by revelation and illumination of the Holy Spirit. Here are some Biblical examples of a word of knowledge.

Acts 5: 1-11
But a certain man named Ananias, with Sapphira his wife, sold a possession.

² And he kept back *part* of the proceeds, his wife also being aware *of it,* and brought a certain part and laid *it* at the apostles' feet. ³ But Peter said, "Ananias, why has Satan filled your heart to lie to the Holy Spirit and keep back *part* of the price of the land for yourself? ⁴ While it remained, was it not your own? And after it was sold, was it not in your own control? Why have you conceived this thing in your heart? You have not lied to men but to God."⁵ Then Ananias, hearing these words, fell down and breathed his last. So great fear came upon all those who heard these things. ⁶ And the young men arose and wrapped him up, carried *him* out, and buried *him.*⁷ Now it was about three hours later when his wife came in, not knowing what had happened. ⁸ And Peter answered her, "Tell me whether you sold the land for so much? "She said, "Yes, for so much." ⁹ Then Peter said to her, "How is it that you have agreed together to test the Spirit of the Lord? Look, the feet of those who have buried your husband *are* at the door, and they will carry you out." ¹⁰ Then immediately she fell down at his feet and breathed her last. And the young men came in and found her dead, and carrying *her* out, buried *her* by her husband. ¹¹ So great fear came upon all the church and upon all who heard these things.

John 4: 7-18
⁷ A woman of Samaria came to draw water. Jesus said to her, "Give Me a drink." ⁸ For His disciples had gone away into the city to buy food.⁹ Then the woman of Samaria said to Him, "How is it that You, being a Jew, ask a drink from me, a Samaritan woman?" For Jews have no dealings with Samaritans.¹⁰ Jesus answered and said to her, "If you knew the gift of God, and who it is who says to you, 'Give Me a drink,' you would have asked Him, and He would have given you living water."

¹¹ The woman said to Him, "Sir, You have nothing to draw with, and the well is deep. Where then do You get that living water? ¹² Are You greater than our father Jacob, who gave us the well, and drank from it himself, as well as his sons and his livestock?" ¹³ Jesus answered and said to her, "Whoever drinks of this water will thirst again, ¹⁴ but whoever drinks of the water that I shall give him will never thirst. But the water that I shall give him will become in him a fountain of water springing up into everlasting life." ¹⁵ The woman said to Him, "Sir, give me this water, that I may not thirst, nor come here to draw." ¹⁶ Jesus said to her, "Go, call your husband, and come here." ¹⁷ The woman answered and said, "I have no husband." Jesus said to her, "You have well said, 'I have no husband,' ¹⁸ for you have had five husbands, and the one whom you now have is not your husband; in that you spoke truly."

The purpose of a Word of Knowledge is:
1. To effectively counsel someone. A word of knowledge reveals a person's root problems. A word of knowledge reveals the secrets of people's hearts in order to help them, not abuse or manipulate them.
2. To reveal sickness or disease
3. To reveal satanic oppression or possession
4. To reveal how to pray for someone.

Revelation about the future
Prophecy is the foretelling of future events uttered through the spoken word, written word and songs. All of the following methods of prophesying can be released through the spoken word, the written word and songs.

Personal Prophecy
Personal prophecy is prophecy to an individual that is personal in nature and meant only for that person. Most personal prophecies are conditional.

Guidelines to receiving personal prophecy.
It is always a good idea for the prophet to communicate the following guidelines to the recipients of the prophecy.

A. Listen attentively during the prophecy to what is being said to you.
B. If the prophecy is not being recorded, immediately write it down afterwards.
C. Go over your recorded prophecies carefully.
D. Inquire of the Lord as to whether it is indeed a word from Him. False prophecies have been spoken over people that have caused much hurt and anguish because the recipient of the prophecy did not find out if it was indeed a word from God..
E. Ask the Lord for clarity where it is needed.
F. Note carefully if there were any instructions in the prophecy that the Lord wants you to follow.
G. Most personal prophecies are conditional. Are there any conditions that must be fulfilled before the prophecy can come to pass?
H. Pray and war over your prophecies.
I. Declare (pronounce, speak out) and Decree (proclaim, command). That is, speak out the prophecy as though it has already happened.

J. Remember that prophecies are fulfilled in God's timing, not yours. Do not become discouraged if the prophecy is not fulfilled in your time! Sometimes the Lord will give a specific time period in which the prophecy will be fulfilled. It may take a long time for some prophecies to come to pass.

K. Guard your prophecies carefully. Use godly wisdom as to if, when and with whom you should share your prophecy.

L. Stand in faith believing that what God has said will come to pass.

Corporate Prophecy

The word corporate means relating to a large company or group (Dictionary.com, 2013). Corporate prophecies are prophecies for groups such as Churches, a nation, nations, governments and other organizations.

Edification

Prophecies of edification build up, instruct and improve people's lives.

Exhortation

Prophecies of exhortation are those that beseech and admonish a person to pursue a specific course of conduct.

Comfort

Prophecies of comfort soothe, console and encourage people who are sad and experiencing deep grief. Such prophecies provide the person with solace (comfort and consolation in a time of distress or sadness).

Direction
Prophecies of direction reveal to people the way they should go or proceed in matters such as marriage, ministry, business, education, careers and relocation.

Instruction
Prophecies of instruction are meant to guide, teach and counsel someone in order for them to learn how to conduct themselves in specific situations. They are also meant to alter the person's course when they have gone astray.

Warning
Prophecies of warning warn and reprimand someone firmly.

Correction
Prophecies of correction chastise someone to make them understand that they have failed or done something wrong. God chastises people so that they can change or improve their behavior. God chastises the heathen, but also chastises those that are His sons and daughters.

Prophetic Preaching
Prophetic preaching is when God uses someone to preach the exact message he wants the person to preach at a specific place and time and to a specific person, people or organization. The preacher must always seek the Lord regarding what he wants him to preach and should **not** preach what he wants to preach. Preaching must always be divine revelation from the Lord. The preacher must not compromise to please the people he is

preaching to, or the person who invited him to preach at their Church, ministry, event or outreach meeting. God uses preaching to communicate what is on his heart (his feelings and his emotions). Prophetic preaching should be any or all of the following as the Lord directs-edification, exhortation, comfort, encouragement, direction, instruction, correction, judgment and warning.

Prophetic Intercession
The prophet must always be led by the Holy Spirit, even when interceding in prayer. Intercession means to intervene and plead on behalf of a person, place, situation or problem. Intercession must not come from the soul. The soul consists of the mind, the will, and the emotions. Your mind is the part of your soul that thinks, reasons and formulates ideas. Your will is the part of your soul that makes choices - good and bad. Your emotions are that part of your soul that make you feel a certain things. Emotions are strong feelings which originate from one's circumstances, mood, or relationships with other people. Intercession must not be what you think and feel according to your judgment and analysis of what should be prayed. The prophet must receive and apply the revelation of the Lord when in intercession.. Using that foundation, the prophecy is embodied and released in the intercession, and the prophet can then pour out his soul in intercession as led by the Holy Spirit.

Psalm 42: 1-4-Amplified
[1] As the deer pants [longingly] for the water brooks,
So my soul pants [longingly] for You, O God. [2] My soul (my life, my inner self) thirsts for God, for the living God. When will I come and see the face of God? [3] My tears have been my food day and night, While they say to me all day long, "Where is your God?"[4] These things I [vividly] remember as I pour out my soul

1 Samuel 1: 1-17

Now there was a certain man of Ramathaim Zophim, of the mountains of Ephraim, and his name *was* Elkanah the son of Jeroham, the son of Elihu, the son of Tohu, the son of Zuph, an Ephraimite. ²And he had two wives: the name of one *was* Hannah, and the name of the other Peninnah. Peninnah had children, but Hannah had no children. ³This man went up from his city yearly to worship and sacrifice to the Lord of hosts in Shiloh. Also the two sons of Eli, Hophni and Phinehas, the priests of the Lord, *were* there. ⁴And whenever the time came for Elkanah to make an offering, he would give portions to Peninnah his wife and to all her sons and daughters. ⁵But to Hannah he would give a double portion, for he loved Hannah, although the Lord had closed her womb. ⁶And her rival also provoked her severely, to make her miserable, because the Lord had closed her womb. ⁷So it was, year by year, when she went up to the house of the Lord, that she provoked her; therefore she wept and did not eat. ⁸Then Elkanah her husband said to her, "Hannah, why do you weep? Why do you not eat? And why is your heart grieved? *Am* I not better to you than ten sons?" ⁹So Hannah arose after they had finished eating and drinking in Shiloh. Now Eli the priest was sitting on the seat by the doorpost of the tabernacle of the Lord. ¹⁰And she *was* in bitterness of soul, and prayed to the Lord and wept in anguish. ¹¹Then she made a vow and said, "O Lord of hosts, if You will indeed look on the affliction of Your maidservant and remember me, and not forget Your maidservant, but will give Your maidservant a male child, then I will give him to the Lord all the days of his life, and no razor shall come upon his head." ¹²And it happened, as she continued praying before the Lord, that Eli watched her mouth. ¹³ Now Hannah spoke in her heart; only her lips moved, but her voice was not heard. Therefore Eli thought she was drunk. ¹⁴ So Eli said to her, "How long will you be drunk? Put your wine away from you!" ¹⁵ But Hannah answered and said, "No, my lord, I *am* a woman of sorrowful spirit. I have drunk neither wine nor intoxicating drink, but have poured out my soul before the Lord. ¹⁶ Do not consider your maidservant a wicked woman, for out of the abundance of my complaint and grief I have spoken until now." ¹⁷ Then Eli answered and said, "Go in peace, and the God of Israel grant your petition which you have asked of Him."

Prophesying in Tongues

A prophecy is often expressed in tongues. However, it should always be followed by the interpretation of tongues. The interpretation of tongues is a spiritual gift. The person releasing the prophecy in tongues can also be the interpreter.

1 Corinthians 12:7-10

⁷ But the manifestation of the Spirit is given to each one for the profit *of all:* ⁸ for to one is given the word of wisdom through the Spirit, to another the word of knowledge through the same Spirit, ⁹ to another faith by the same Spirit, to another gifts of healings by the same Spirit, ¹⁰ to another the working of miracles, to another prophecy, to another discerning of spirits, to another *different* kinds of tongues, to another the interpretation of tongues.

Chapter 7
Prophetic Worship

The Lord uses the prophet to prophesy in song. This is called prophetic worship. Prophetic worship can be songs that are already written or spontaneous songs. The type of prophet that prophesies in song is called a prophetic psalmist. The prophet must clearly understand what true worship really is.

What is worship?
Worship begins in the heart, and manifests through your words and actions. Worship is to adore and love the Lord with all your heart. True worship, that is acceptable to the Lord, is to have a passionate desire in your heart to please the Lord in everything you say, do or think. It means to pant after God; to hunger and thirst after him; to want His perfect will in every area of your life; to love Him more than anyone or anything, and to reverence Him. Everything you do, say or think should be an act of worship unto the Lord. A person can exhibit the physical motions and not be worshiping the Lord. God sees the heart. He craves and deserves sincere, heartfelt worship. Praise is part of worship. Praise is celebratory and worship is deeper, meditative and more intimate. Worship is for an audience of one-the Lord God, almighty.

> **John 4:23 -Amplified**
> A time will come, however, indeed it is already here, when the true (genuine) worshipers will worship the Father in spirit and in truth (reality); for the Father is seeking just such people as these as His worshipers.

The following definitions of worship are taken from Strong's Greek and Hebrew Lexicon.

Greek
Sebomai: to revere, to adore

Revere means to regard as worthy of great honor. Adore means loving admiration and devotion

Latreuo: to minister to the Lord;

Proskuneo: to prostrate oneself.

Hebrew
Shachah: to prostrate in homage to the Lord.

To prostrate means "to stretch out with face on the ground in adoration or submission" (Dictionary.com, 2013). Worship, therefore, means to minister to the Lord and stretch out with your face on the ground in adoration or submission in homage (an expression of high regard) to God.

Worship in The Old Testament
The Tabernacle of Moses
In the Tabernacle of Moses, the offering up of a sacrifice was a prophetic act symbolizing the perfect and final sacrifice of Jesus Christ, the spotless Lamb of God whose blood was shed for the remission of our sins. Old Testament sacrifices had to be done in a precise way that was acceptable unto the Lord or the Lord would reject the sacrifice.

The Mosaic Tabernacle
Acceptable Sacrifices

The priests entered through the door into the Tabernacle's Outer Court. They had to wash their hands and feet at the Laver before they could either enter into the Sanctuary Building or make any offering to the Lord at the Burnt Offering Altar. God warned Moses that if the priests did not wash they would die (Exodus 30:20-21).

The blood sacrifice had to be a male lamb without any defects or blemishes. The animal had to be killed in the outer court of the Tabernacle and prepared a specific way. The blood had to be sprinkled a specific way and the fire had to be prepared a specific way. When done the Lord's way, it became an acceptable sacrifice unto the Lord. The aroma (a distinctive pervasive and usually pleasant or savory smell) ascended up to God and it was soothing and pleasing to Him.

Exodus 29:15-17
[15] "You shall also take one ram, and Aaron and his sons shall put their hands on the head of the ram; [16] and you shall kill the ram, and you shall take its blood and sprinkle it all around on the altar. [17] Then you shall cut the ram in pieces, wash its entrails and its legs, and put them with its pieces and with its head.

¹⁸ And you shall burn the whole ram on the altar. It is a burnt offering to the Lord; it is a sweet aroma, an offering made by fire to the Lord.

Sacrifices of Praise and Worship

We are to bring sacrifices of praise to the Lord. A sacrifice is an act of offering something precious to God.

Hebrews 13:15
¹⁵ Therefore by Him let us continually offer the sacrifice of praise to God, that is, the fruit of *our* lips, giving thanks to His name.

Psalm 27:6
Amplified Bible
⁶ And now shall my head be lifted up above my enemies round about me; in His tent I will offer sacrifices and shouting of joy; I will sing, yes, I will sing praises to the Lord.

Psalm 54:6
I will freely sacrifice to You;
I will praise Your name, O Lord, for *it is* good.

John 4:24
God *is* Spirit, and those who worship Him must worship in spirit and truth."

Worship is a sacrifice that we must offer up to God daily. There are so many misinterpretations of what it really means to bring sacrifices of praise and worship to God. Many believe it means that you must give up yourself and your time, put things and people aside, and praise God when you don't feel like it.

And it's true that you must do those things. But a sacrifice of worship has to do with the quality of the worship that you offer up to the Lord.

Unacceptable Sacrifices in the Bible
If the sacrifice was not done the right way it was unacceptable to the Lord and He rejected it. In the book of Malachi, the Lord admonishes Israel for defiling the altar of God by presenting polluted offerings to Him.

> **Malachi 1:6-8**
> ⁶ "A son honors his father, And a servant his master. If then I am the Father, Where is My honor? And if I am a Master, Where is My reverence? Says the Lord of hosts To you priests who despise My name. Yet you say, 'In what way have we despised Your name?' ⁷ "You offer defiled food on My altar, But say, 'In what way have we defiled You?' By saying, 'The table of the Lord is [a]contemptible.' ⁸ And when you offer the blind as a sacrifice, Is it not evil? And when you offer the lame and sick, Is it not evil? Offer it then to your governor! Would he be pleased with you? Would he accept[b] you favorably?" Says the Lord of hosts.

Nadab and Abihu offended the Lord by offering up strange fire to the Lord and God rejected it.

> **Leviticus 10:1-3**
> ¹⁰ Then Nadab and Abihu, the sons of Aaron, each took his censer and put fire in it, put incense on it, and offered profane fire before the Lord, which He had not commanded them. ² So fire went out from the Lord and devoured them, and they died before the Lord.

³ And Moses said to Aaron, "This is what the Lord spoke, saying: 'By those who come near Me I must be regarded as holy; And before all the people. I must be glorified". So Aaron held his peace.

As you offer up sacrifices of worship unto the Lord, it must be acceptable. You must purify your heart- repent of all sin); get rid of habitual sins; remove all demonic influences; be free from emotional bondages and everything that would hinder you from bringing sacrifices of worship unto the Lord. You must not present any "strange fire" unto the Lord because He will not accept your worship. Are you living right? Are you holy and godly in everything you say, do or think? Are you serving two masters?

> **Matthew 6: 24. Amplified**
> ²⁴ "No one can serve two masters; for either he will hate the one and love the other, or he will be devoted to the one and despise the other. You cannot serve God and mammon [money, possessions, fame, status, or whatever is valued more than the Lord].

Is there someone or something that you love more than God? That is strange fire. That is profane fire. And that is not an acceptable sacrifice of worship unto the Lord. Your sacrifice of worship should be a sweet-smelling aroma unto the Lord and not a stench in His nostrils. Your worship and praise must be based on holiness, reverence and adoration unto the Lord.

> **Psalm 29:1-3**
> *A Psalm of David.*
> ²⁹ Give unto the Lord, O you mighty ones,
> Give unto the Lord glory and strength.

> [2] Give unto the Lord the glory due to His name;
> Worship the Lord in the beauty of holiness.

Worship begins in the heart and is expressed or manifested through physical activities. When you are a true worshipper, you can't sit still. You **will** manifest (make visible) the worship that is in your heart. Here are some manifestations of worship:

- Singing
- Clapping
- Playing musical instruments
- Dancing
- Kneeling
- Extending your hands
- Shouting
- Jumping
- Weeping

Worship, and its manifestations, must be prophetic and patterned after Davidic Worship. Davidic Worship refers to the type of worship that was instituted by David in the Old Testament before the birth of the Messiah, Jesus Christ. David was a king of Israel, a priest, a mighty warrior, a worshipper and musician, a shepherd a prophet and a man after God's own heart". Davidic worship is prophetic worship. It is true worship unto Jehovah that is celebratory, jubilant and passionate. It is the kind of worship where no one is inhibited (self-conscious). It is pure worship that is lifted up to God without any thought in the minds of the worshippers about how foolish they behaved and looked or if they would be criticized by others.

In Amos 9:10-12, the Lord spoke through the prophet Amos that in the last days He would restore The Tabernacle of David. The rebuilding of the tabernacle refers to the restoration of the praise and worship that took place in the Tabernacle of David.

The Tabernacle of David was a simple tent that David erected to have 24-hour worship unto the Lord. There was nothing fancy about the tabernacle. It was just a plain ordinary tent, but what took place inside it was extraordinary!

It was just a simple tent, but The Ark of God which represented the presence of God -the very Glory of God- dwelled inside the tent. David appointed four thousand men to praise the Lord with musical instruments. That was their job. They did nothing else. There was 24-hour corporate worship and praise unto the Lord in the Tabernacle of David. There were singers, dancers, musicians. There was rejoicing, celebration, and adoration unto the Lord. The worship was vibrant and pure.. According to history, the worship in the Tabernacle of David went on for 36 years!

1 Chronicles 15:16
[16] Then David spoke to the leaders of the Levites to appoint their brethren *to be* the singers accompanied by instruments of music, stringed instruments, harps, and cymbals, by raising the voice with resounding joy.

1 Chronicles 16:4-6

⁴ And he appointed some of the Levites to minister before the ark of the Lord, to commemorate, to thank, and to praise the Lord God of Israel: ⁵ Asaph the chief, and next to him Zechariah, *then* Jeiel, Shemiramoth, Jehiel, Mattithiah, Eliab, Benaiah, and Obed-Edom: Jeiel with stringed instruments and harps, but Asaph made music with cymbals; ⁶ Benaiah and Jahaziel the priests regularly *blew* the trumpets before the ark of the covenant of God.

> I Chronicles 24 and 25 lists the divisions and the responsibilities for worship in The Tabernacle of David

The Lord is restoring Davidic worship, the type of worship in the Tabernacle of David. Davidic worship is prophetic worship. Prophetic worship accomplishes a multitude of things.

- Prophetic worship communicates the heart, thoughts and desires of the Lord.
- Prophetic worship creates an atmosphere for the visitation of the Holy Spirit.
- Prophetic worship releases the Glory of God.
- Prophetic worship breaks open the atmosphere for the Lord to move freely.
- Prophetic worship creates an atmosphere for signs, wonders and miracles to manifest.
- People get healed and delivered from strongholds.
- Prophetic worship tears down the strongholds of darkness.
- Prophetic worship opens doors.
- Prophetic worship brings change.

- Prophetic worship releases blessings.
- Prophetic worship creates an atmosphere for intimacy with the Lord
- Prophetic worship impacts cities and nations

Psalms
One of the Hebrew words for psalm is Mizmowr *(pronounced miz-more)* which means a poem set to notes. A psalm is a prophetic song which is usually accompanied by a musical instrument. The psalms in the Bible were produced by a variety of psalmists. Seventy-three of the psalms are ascribed to David. David wrote most of the Psalms when he was being persecuted by Saul. True praise and worship is birthed out of extreme experiences that are usually painful.

Homework Assignment
Write a prophetic psalm.

Spontaneous Prophetic Songs
Spontaneous prophetic songs are songs that are unknown and have not been written or recorded. They are led by the Holy Spirit and seem like they are being made up as the person is singing. But they are not made-up songs. They flow out from the depths of the person as the Spirit of the Lord overshadows them and fills them. The Greek word for overshadow is episkiazo (pronounced *ep-ee-skee-ad'-zo*) which means: to envelop in a haze of brilliancy; to empower with supernatural influence.

Genres (Types) of Prophetic Songs
The Song of The Lord
The Song of the Lord is an inspired prophetic song of praise, worship and adoration directed and sung to the Church and to

the Father. A prophetic song (prophecy in song) has the same purpose of prophecy.

2 Chronicles 29:27
²⁷ Then Hezekiah commanded *them* to offer the burnt offering on the altar. And when the burnt offering began, the song of the Lord *also* began, with the trumpets and with the instruments of David king of Israel.

Here are some Biblical examples of the Song of the Lord to the Church and to the Father.

The Song of the Lord to the Church
Psalm 149: 1-3
Praise the Lord!
Sing to the Lord a new song,
And His praise in the assembly of saints.
² Let Israel rejoice in their Maker;
Let the children of Zion be joyful in their King.
³ Let them praise His name with the dance;
Let them sing praises to Him with the timbrel and harp

The Song of the Lord to the Father
Psalm 96:2-5
Amplified Bible
² Sing to the Lord, bless His name;
Proclaim good news of His salvation from day to day.
³ Declare His glory among the nations, His marvelous works and wonderful deeds among all the peoples.
4 For great is the Lord and greatly to be praised;
He is to be feared above all gods.
5 For all the gods of the peoples are [worthless, lifeless] idols, But the Lord made the heaven

Zephaniah 3:17
Amplified Bible
[17] "The Lord your God is in your midst,
A Warrior who saves.
He will rejoice over you with joy;
He will be quiet in His love [making no mention of your past sins],
He will rejoice over you with shouts of joy.

The Song of the Bridegroom
The Song of the Bridegroom is a love song by Jesus, the bridegroom, to the bride. It is much like the Song of The Lord but is much more intimate in nature where Jesus sings a love song to His Bride. A Song of the Bride (response to the Song of the Bridegroom) usually follows the song of the Bridegroom.

The Song of The Bride
The Song of the Bride is an inspired prophetic song in response to the Song of The Bridegroom. The following definition of the Bride is by Robert Gay, worship leader and Pastor of Prophetic Praise Ministries. *"The Song of the Bride is a song of love and adoration in response to the Song of the Bridegroom. This song is responsive in nature as the bride expresses to the bridegroom her love for him. It is usually intimate in nature and enables the Church to express by the Spirit of God the depth of love she has for the bridegroom, Jesus".*

The Song of Deliverance
The Song of Deliverance is an inspired prophetic song of deliverance, healing and restoration.

Jeremiah 30: 17
For I will restore health to you
And heal you of your wounds,' says the Lord,

'Because they called you an outcast saying:
"This is Zion;
  No one seeks her."

The Song of War

The Song of War is an inspired prophetic song of war.

Isaiah 30:30-31

[30] The Lord will cause His glorious voice to be heard,
And show the descent of His arm,
With the indignation of *His* anger
And the flame of a devouring fire,
With scattering, tempest, and hailstones.
31 For through the voice of the Lord
Assyria will be [a]beaten down,
As He strikes with the rod.

Chapter 8
A Company of Prophets

In Biblical times, "schools of the prophets", were instituted for the training of prophets. These "schools" were established at Ramah, Bethel, Gilgal, Gibeah, and Jericho. According to Easton's 1897 Bible Dictionary, these young men were taught not only the fundamentals of secular knowledge, but they were taught how to exercise the office of prophet which was "to preach pure morality and the heart-felt worship of Jehovah, and to act along and co-coordinately with the priesthood and monarchy in guiding the state aright and checking all attempts at illegality and tyranny." (Easton's Bible Dictionary, 2021)

These young men were called the sons of the prophets. The phrase, the sons of the prophets, is mentioned 11 times in the Bible.

> **2 Kings 2:7 AMP**
> [7] Fifty men of the sons of the prophets also went and stood opposite them [to watch] at a distance; and the two of them stood by the Jordan.

> **2 Kings 4:1 AMP**
> [1] Now one of the wives of a man of the sons of the prophets cried out to Elisha [for help], saying "Your servant my husband is dead, and you know that your servant [reverently] feared the LORD; but the creditor is coming to take my two sons to be his slaves [in payment for a loan]."

The sons of the prophets were young men who lived together at these different schools under the tutelage and mentorship of a senior prophet who was the prophet's spiritual father. These sons of the prophets were taught, trained, equipped and nurtured by these spiritual fathers who were mature and seasoned prophets. They imparted what was on their lives into the lives of their spiritual sons. Impartation means to transfer something to someone else. Impartation is done through training, equipping and the laying on of hands. Elisha the prophet was the "son" of Elijah the prophet. Before Elijah was taken up into heaven, he imparted a double portion of his spirit into the life of his "son" Elisha.

2 Kings 2:3
[3] Now the sons of the prophets who *were* at Bethel came out to Elisha, and said to him, "Do you know that the Lord will take away your master from over you today?" And he said, "Yes, I know; keep silent!"

2 Kings 2:9-14 AMP
[9] And when they had crossed over, Elijah said to Elisha, "Ask what I shall do for you before I am taken from you." And Elisha said, "Please let a double portion of your spirit be upon me." [10] He said, "You have asked for a difficult thing. However, if you see me when I am taken from you, it shall be so for you; but if not, it shall not be so." [11] As they continued along and talked, behold, a chariot of fire with horses of fire [appeared suddenly and] separated the two of them, and Elijah went up to heaven in a whirlwind. [12] Elisha saw it and cried out, "My father, my father, the chariot of Israel and its horsemen!" And he no longer saw Elijah. Then he took hold of his own clothes and tore them into two pieces [in grief].

[13] He picked up the mantle of Elijah that fell off him, and went back and stood by the bank of the Jordan. [14] He took the mantle of Elijah that fell from him and struck the waters and said, "Where is the LORD, the God of Elijah?" And when he too had struck the waters, they divided this way and that, and Elisha crossed over.

The sons of the prophets and their spiritual fathers were a company, or group, of prophets who lived together, ate together and prophesied together. They had a close bond of unity.

2 Kings 4:38
38 And Elisha returned to Gilgal, and *there was* a famine in the land. Now the sons of the prophets *were* sitting before him; and he said to his servant, "Put on the large pot, and boil stew for the sons of the prophets.

1 Samuel 10:5-6
5 After that you will come to the hill of God where the garrison of the Philistines is; and when you come there to the city, you will meet a group of prophets coming down from the high place [of worship] with harp, tambourine, flute, and lyre before them, and they will be prophesying. 6 Then the Spirit of the Lord will come upon you mightily, and you will prophesy with them, and you will be changed into another man.

The word company means-"the fact or condition of being with another or others, especially in a way that provides friendship and enjoyment" (Dictionary.com, 2013).
Two Hebrew words for company are:

1. Gduwd *(pronounced ghed-ood')* which means- a crowd of soldiers; army; band; troop.

2. Chayil*(pronounced khah'-yil)* which means- a force; an army; virtue; valor; strength; a band of soldiers; great forces; power; strength; war.

In Greek, the word "group" is patria *(pronounced pat-ree-ah')* which means -a group of families; kindred. The words "company" and "group" and their Hebrew and Greek meanings symbolize the importance and role of the company of prophets in the Old Testament and in the present times. God is raising up a company of prophets that are a type of the Old Testament prophets. They will be the *Gduwd*, the *Chayil* and the *Patria*. They will, as the Old Testament prophets did, enjoy each other's friendship. They will have a strong bond of unity. They will have and develop a strong kinship with each other. They will be a strong, mighty and powerful army of accurate prophets who will not compromise, and who will live holy and righteous before the Lord. They will be as iron sharpening iron. The phrase "iron sharpens iron" is found in Proverbs 27:17:
"As iron sharpens iron, so one man sharpens and influences another." When two iron blades are rubbed together, the edges become sharper, which makes the blades to more efficiently cut and slice. Likewise, as the prophets work together as a team, each one sharpens the other one as they prophesy together and interact with each other.

Question:
Why is important to have a school of prophets?
_____
_____

Who were the sons of the prophets?

Chapter 9
The Prophet's Mandate

A mandate is an official order and commission to do something. A mandate is usually given by a person or government with a very high level of authority to an elected group of people, to perform an action on behalf of the person or government. God, who has supreme authority, and who governs heaven and earth has given a mandate to his prophets, an elected (chosen) group of people, to execute.

In general, the prophet's mandate is "to preach pure morality and the heart-felt worship of Jehovah" (Easton's Bible Dictionary, 2021), to guide the Church and States aright and check all attempts at illegality and tyranny.

Specifically, the Prophet's Mandate is :

1. To prophesy the word of the Lord without compromise. To compromise is to lower your principles, beliefs, standards and morals in order to be accepted by someone or society.

> **Proverbs 25:26 AMP**
> [26] Like a muddied fountain and a polluted spring Is a righteous man who yields and compromises his integrity before the wicked.

1 John 5:21 AMP
[21] Little children (believers, dear ones), guard yourselves from idols-[false teachings, moral compromises, and anything that would take God's place in your heart].

There is an account in the Bible of a prophet from Judah whom God commanded to go to Bethel and prophesy against an idolatrous altar in the presence of King Jeroboam. Jeroboam was an evil and idolatrous king who erected golden calves which he set up as symbols of Jehovah, ordering the people to no longer go up to worship at Jerusalem, but to bring their offerings to the shrines he had erected. While Jeroboam was offering incense at Bethel, the prophet whom the Lord sent from Judah appeared before him with a warning message from the Lord. Jeroboam became angry and attempted to arrest the prophet but his hand was "dried up," and the altar before which he stood was rent asunder. This account is given in 1 Kings, Chapter 13.

1 Kings 13:1-32 AMP
[1] Now behold, there came a man of God from Judah to Bethel by the word (command) of the LORD, while Jeroboam was standing by the altar [which he had built] to burn incense. [2] The man cried out against the [idolatrous] altar by the word of the LORD, "O altar, altar, thus says the Lord: 'Behold, a son shall be born to the house of David, Josiah by name; and on you shall he sacrifice [the bodies of] the priests of the high places who burn incense on you, and human bones shall be burned on you.'" [3] And he gave a sign the same day, saying, "This is the sign which the LORD has spoken: 'Behold, the altar shall be split apart and the ashes that are on it shall be poured out.'"

[4] When the king heard the words which the man of God cried out against the altar in Bethel, Jeroboam put out his hand from the altar, saying, "Seize him!" And his hand which he had put out against him withered, so that he was unable to pull it back to himself. [5] The altar also was split apart and the ashes were poured out from the altar in accordance with the sign which the man of God had given by the word of the LORD. [6] The king answered and said to the man of God, "Please entreat [the favor of] the LORD your God and pray for me, that my hand may be restored to me." So the man of God entreated the LORD, and the king's hand was restored to him and became as it was before. [7] And the king said to the man of God, "Come home with me and refresh yourself, and I will give you a reward." [8] But the man of God said to the king, "Even if you were to give me half your house (wealth), I would not go with you, nor would I eat bread or drink water in this place. [9] For I was commanded by the word of the LORD, 'You shall not eat bread or drink water, nor shall you return by the way you came.'" [10] So he went another way and did not return by the way that he came to Bethel. [11] Now there was an old prophet living in Bethel; and his sons came and told him everything that the man of God had done that day in Bethel; they also told their father the words which he had spoken to the king. [12] Their father asked them, "Which way did he go?" For his sons had seen which way the man of God who came from Judah had gone. [13] He said to his sons, "Saddle the donkey for me." So they saddled the donkey for him and he rode away on it, [14] and he went after the man of God. And he found him sitting under an oak (terebinth) tree, and he said to him, "Are you the man of God who came from Judah?" And he said, "I am." [15] Then he said to him, "Come home with me and eat bread."

" [16] He said, "I cannot return with you nor go in with you, nor will I eat bread or drink water with you in this place. [17] For I was told by the word of the LORD, 'You shall not eat bread nor drink water there, nor shall you return by going the way that you came.'" [18] He answered him, "I too am a prophet, as you are; and an angel spoke to me by the word of the LORD, saying, 'Bring him back with you to your house, so that he may eat bread and drink water.'" But he lied to him. [19] So the man of God went back with him, and ate bread in his house and drank water.

> *The prophet must always speak and do what God says without compromise regardless of who tells the prophet to act and speak contrary to what the Lord has directed him to. The Lord will always hold the prophet responsible for delivering the prophetic word. He must not allow himself to be influenced by anyone to disobey God or he will suffer the consequences.*

[20] Now it happened as they were sitting at the table, that the word of the LORD came to the prophet who had brought him back. [21] And he cried out to the man of God who had come from Judah, "Thus says the LORD, 'Because you have disobeyed the word of the LORD and have not kept the commandment which the LORD your God commanded you, [22] but have come back and have eaten bread and drunk water in the place of which the LORD said to you, "You shall not eat bread nor drink water"; your body shall not come to the tomb of your fathers (ancestors).'" [23] After the prophet of the house had eaten bread and after he had drunk, he saddled the donkey for the prophet whom he had brought back. [24] Now when he had gone, a lion met him by the road

and killed him, and his body was thrown in the road, with the donkey standing beside it; the lion was also standing beside the body. [25] And there were men passing by, and they saw the body thrown in the road, and the lion standing beside the body. So they came and told about it in the city [of Bethel] where the old prophet lived. [26] When the prophet who had brought him back from the road heard about it, he said, "It is the man of God who was disobedient to the word of the LORD; therefore the LORD has given him to the lion, which has torn him and killed him, in accordance with the word of the LORD which He spoke to him." [27] And he said to his sons, "Saddle the donkey for me." And they saddled it. [28] And he went and found the body thrown on the road, and the donkey and the lion standing beside the body; the lion [miraculously] had not eaten the body or attacked the donkey. [29] Then the prophet picked up the body of the man of God and laid it on the donkey and brought it back, and he came into the city (Bethel) of the old prophet to mourn and to bury him. [30] And he laid the body in his own grave, and they mourned over him, saying, "Alas, my brother!" [31] Then after he had buried him, he said to his sons, "When I am dead, bury me in the grave in which the man of God is buried; lay my bones beside his bones. [32] For the words which he cried out by the word of the LORD against the altar in Bethel and against all the houses of the high places which are in the cities of Samaria shall certainly come to pass."

People who compromise (lower their standards , morals principles and beliefs) are people-pleasers. People-pleasers are people who are afraid of being rejected. Rejection comes with being a prophet. People reject the prophet if they do not like the word they prophesy.

The prophet is also rejected when the enemy influences people to reject them. The Old Testament prophets were stoned. Stoning was a capital punishment as a result of sin. Some sins that resulted in stoning in the Old Testament were murder, idolatry, adultery, fornication, witchcraft, necromancy and blasphemy. Prophets in the Bible were stoned for "perceived" blasphemy because the rebellious folks of the day did not want to change.

As they stoned the prophets of old, so too are present day prophets stoned, not with stones but with harsh words. They are stoned with rejection. They are stoned with slander. They are stoned with evil criticisms. They are stoned with evil judgments and pronouncements.

The prophet should always be a God -pleaser and not a people-pleaser.

Signs That You Are a People-Pleaser

You agree with everyone and everything
You pretend to agree with things you really do not agree with because you want to be liked.

You apologize very often.
You blame yourself for things you did not say or do, and feel the need to apologize even if you are blameless. You also apologize frequently because of self-rejection and low self-esteem issues. Frequent apologizing is also because you are constantly afraid that people are blaming you.

Partners and friends become frustrated with you
Your partner and friends usually notice the way you agree with everyone and everything and become frustrated with what you are doing. It also causes them to reject you because they see you as a weak, spineless (weak or cowardly) person.

People take advantage of you
Some people take advantage of you because they see you are a weak, spineless people-pleaser.

You take on more than you are able to do
Because you want to please others, you take on projects and activities that you think other people want you to do.

You find it hard to say "no"
You say yes to almost everything people ask you to do. In the middle of the project, you may back out of it because you feel you are inadequate. You do this by making excuses such as "I am not feeling well" or "I have something to do on that day".

You feel uncomfortable if someone is angry with you, or appears to be angry with you.
You hate the thought of someone being angry with you, so in order to gain their approval, you compromise your values. You also perceive that someone is angry with you when actually they are actually not. You believe they are angry because of the rejection you have suffered.

You behave like the people around you.
You behave the way other people behave, or the way they want you to behave. This results in loss of identity. You often feel that you do not know who you really are.

You need to be complimented so that you can feel good about yourself

The need to be complimented in order to feel good about yourself is because of low self-esteem and low self-worth. People pleasers draw their self-worth from the approval of others.

2. Obedience

To be obedient means to submit to the authority of someone or comply with a law. It also means to carry out (a command or instruction) (Dictionary.com, 2013)

The Greek word for obedience is <u>hupakoe</u> (*pronounced hoop-ak-o-ay'*). It means compliance and submission.

Acts 5:29 AMP
Then Peter and the apostles replied, "We must obey God rather than men [we have no other choice].

3. Honesty and Integrity

There is a correlation between honesty and integrity. Honesty is "truthfulness, sincerity, or frankness; freedom from deceit or fraud." (Dictionary.com, 2013) Integrity is "adherence to moral and ethical principles; soundness of moral character; honesty." (Dictionary.com, 2013). Honesty means telling the truth, while integrity means having high moral standards, character, ethics and principles. Integrity means doing the right thing, whether or not it benefits you. You can be honest and have no integrity, but you cannot have integrity without honesty.

Proverbs 11:3 AMP
The integrity and moral courage of the upright will guide them, But the crookedness of the treacherous will destroy them.

4. Fearless

To be fearless is to be bold, courageous and unafraid.

2 Timothy 1:7 AMP
For God did not give us a spirit of timidity or cowardice or fear, but [He has given us a spirit] of power and of love and of sound judgment and personal discipline [abilities that result in a calm, well-balanced mind and self-control].

Deuteronomy 31:6 AMP
[6] Be strong and courageous, do not be afraid or tremble in dread before them, for it is the LORD your God who goes with you. He will not fail you or abandon you."

A courageous person is a brave person who is not deterred by danger or pain. Dangerous situations and pain do not stop them from being courageous. Rather they bring out the courage and braveness in the person.

The Greek word for courage is tharrheo *(pronounced thar-hreh'-o)* which means to exercise courage; be bold; have confidence, be confident. The Hebrew word for courage is amats (*pronounced aw-mats'*) which means to be alert, physically (on foot) or mentally in courage; of good courage; steadfastly minded; strong; stronger; establish; fortify; harden; increase; prevail; strengthen (self) ; make strong.

5. Holiness

2 Corinthians 7:1 AMP
Therefore, since we have these [great and wonderful] promises, beloved, let us cleanse ourselves from everything

that contaminates body and spirit, completing holiness [living a consecrated life-a life set apart for God's purpose] in the fear of God.

The word for holy in Hebrew is taher *(pronounced taw-hare)*' which means to be pure (sound, clear, unadulterated; uncontaminated; morally, innocent, clean, cleanse (self), purge, purify. The Old Testament prophets feared God. They walked in holiness and knew that if they did not there would be serious consequences. They saw and knew how God judged Israel for their sins of witchcraft, idolatry and spiritual adultery.

6. Boldness

The word bold in Greek is parrhesiazomai *(pronounced par-hray-see-ad'-zom-ahee)* which means to be frank in utterance; confident in spirit and demeanor, to preach and speak boldly.

Proverbs 28:1 AMP
The wicked flee when no one pursues them, But the righteous are as bold as a lion.

The prophet, as a righteous person, should be bold as a lion.

A lion, the animal, is bold, fearless, confident and relentless in the pursuit of what he seeks (his prey).

7. They prophet should not be greedy

The Greek word for greed is aischrokerdes *(pronounced ahee-skhrok-er-dace')* which means selfish gain, sordid, given to (greedy of filthy lucre).

1 Timothy 3:1-3 AMP
[1] This is a faithful and trustworthy saying: if any man [eagerly] seeks the office of overseer (bishop, superintendent), he desires an excellent task. [2] Now an overseer must be blameless and beyond reproach, the husband of one wife, self-controlled, sensible, respectable, hospitable, able to teach, [3] not addicted to wine, not a bully nor quick-tempered and hot-headed, but gentle and considerate, free from the love of money [not greedy for wealth and its inherent power-financially ethical].

Psalm 119:36 AMP
Incline my heart to Your testimonies And not to dishonest gain and envy.

The prophet should not demand that someone pay them for a prophecy. However it is quite correct and acceptable for someone to voluntarily and cheerfully give the prophet a financial gift without any coercion from the prophet or anyone else.

1 Corinthians 9:1-14
[4] Have we not the right to our food and drink [at the expense of the churches]? [5] Have we not the right to take along with us a believing wife, as do the rest of the apostles and the Lord's brothers and Cephas (Peter)?

⁶ Or is it only Barnabas and I who have no right to stop doing manual labor [in order to support our ministry]? ⁷ [Consider this:] Who at any time serves as a soldier at his own expense? Who plants a vineyard and does not eat its fruit? Or who tends a flock and does not use the milk of the flock? ⁸ Do I say these things only from a man's perspective? Does the Law not endorse the same principles? ⁹ For it is written in the Law of Moses, "You shall not muzzle an ox while it is treading out the grain [to keep it from eating the grain]." Is it [only] for oxen that God cares? ¹⁰ Or does He speak entirely for our sake? Yes, it was written for our sake: The plowman ought to plow in hope, and the thresher to thresh in hope of sharing the harvest. ¹¹ If we have sown [the good seed of] spiritual things in you, is it too much if we reap material things from you? ¹² If others share in this rightful claim over you, do not we even more? However, we did not exercise this right, but we put up with everything so that we will not hinder [the spread of] the good news of Christ. ¹³ Do you not know that those who officiate in the sacred services of the temple eat from the temple [offerings of meat and bread] and those who regularly attend the altar have their share from the [offerings brought to the] altar? ¹⁴ So also [on the same principle] the Lord directed those who preach the gospel to get their living from the gospel.

8. Humility

The Hebrew word for humility is shuwach *(pronounced shoo'-akh)* which means to bow down. In Greek the word humility is praus *(pronounced prah-ooc)* which means meek.

The Oxford dictionary of English defines the word humble as being meek, deferential (respectful), submissive, modest, unassuming, self-deprecating (unpretentious), free from vanity (Oxford Dictionary, 2021). To be humble is to have or show a modest or low estimate of one's importance (Oxford Dictionary, 2021).

James 4:6 AMP

But He gives us more and more grace [through the power of the Holy Spirit to defy sin and live an obedient life that reflects both our faith and our gratitude for our salvation]. Therefore, it says, "GOD IS OPPOSED TO THE PROUD and HAUGHTY, BUT [continually] GIVES [the gift of] GRACE TO THE HUMBLE [who turn away from self-righteousness]."

9. Accountability

Accountability means "an obligation or willingness to accept responsibility or to account for one's actions" Accountable means to be "obligated to explain, justify, and take responsibility for one's actions, and to answer to someone, such as a person with more authority. The state of being accountable is accountability. The word accountable is often used in the context of individuals taking responsibility for their actions" (Dictionary.com, 2013).

The prophet must give an account to God for his actions, his words and his behavior. The prophet should also have a seasoned, mature and wise apostle and prophet to whom they are accountable. This spiritual father or mother should guide, mentor and instruct the prophet to always be teachable, to be able to receive correction, to prophesy accurately, to be responsible for the prophetic words they release, to apologize to others if the prophecy is false and to live a repentant life.

While prophets do suffer intense attacks, there must be no legal right for the enemy to attack the prophet.

> **1 Peter 3:13-17**
> [13] Who is going to harm you if you are eager to do good? [14] But even if you should suffer for what is right, you are blessed. "Do not fear their threats do not be frightened."[[15] But in your hearts revere Christ as Lord. Always be prepared to give an answer to everyone who asks you to give the reason for the hope that you have. But do this with gentleness and respect, [16] keeping a clear conscience, so that those who speak maliciously against your good behavior in Christ may be ashamed of their slander. [17] For it is better, if it is God's will, to suffer for doing good than for doing evil.

There must be no breach in the prophet's life. A breach is an act of breaking or failing to observe a law, agreement, or code of conduct of someone in authority (Oxford Dictionary, 2021) The person in authority is God . A breach is also a gap in a wall, barrier, or defence (Oxford Dictionary, 2021). The prophet must not have a gap through which the enemy can enter and attack.

10. The fruit of the Holy Spirit

Spiritual gifts are freely given by God, but the fruit of the Holy Spirit must be grown.

> **Galatians 5:22-23 AMP**
> [22] But the fruit of the Spirit [the result of His presence within us] is love [unselfish concern for others], joy, [inner] peace, patience [not the ability to wait, but how we act while waiting], kindness, goodness, faithfulness, [23] gentleness, self-control. Against such things there is no law.

Questions:

What is the **general** mandate that God gave to the prophet? Please explain what that means.

_____
_____
_____
_____
_____
_____
_____
_____
_____
_____
_____
_____
_____
_____
_____

Chapter 10
Old Testament prophets
Which type are you?

Very little is said of the following prophets, but mention must be made of them. First, we will look at these lesser known prophets, then we will examine the lives of some of the better known prophets.

Miriam

Miriam, the sister of Moses and Aaron was a prophetess. She features in the history of the Jews' exodus from Egypt.

> **Exodus. 15:20**
> [20] Then Miriam the prophetess, the sister of Aaron, took the timbrel in her hand; and all the women went out after her with timbrels and with dances.

After God triumphantly led Israel through the Red Sea and defeated Pharaoh's army, Miriam led the response to the song of Moses and the children of Israel.

> **Exodus 15:21**
> [21] And Miriam answered them: "Sing to the Lord, For He has triumphed gloriously! The horse and its rider He has thrown into the sea!"

Deborah

Deborah was a prophet and judge and headed the army of Israel.

Judges 4:4-5

⁴Now Deborah, a prophetess, the wife of Lapidoth, was judging Israel at that time. ⁵And she would sit under the palm tree of Deborah between Ramah and Bethel in the mountains of Ephraim. And the children of Israel came up to her for judgment.

Deborah commanded Barak the son of Abinoam and said to him, *"Has not the Lord God of Israel commanded, 'Go and deploy troops at Mount Tabor; take with you ten thousand men of the sons of Naphtali and of the sons of Zebulun;* ⁷ *and against you I will deploy Sisera, the commander of Jabin's army, with his chariots and his multitude at the River Kishon; and I will deliver him into your hand'?"* ⁸ *And Barak said to her, "If you will go with me, then I will go; but if you will not go with me, I will not go!"* **Judges 4: 6-8**

On the day that the Lord defeated Jabin, the king of Canaan in the presence of the children of Israel (Judges 4: 23), Deborah and Barak sang the song of the Lord (Judges 5).

Huldah

Huldah, a prophetess, confirmed the validity of the Book of the Law of the Lord given through Moses.

2 Kings 22:14-20

¹⁴So Hilkiah the priest, Ahikam, Achbor, Shaphan, and Asaiah went to Huldah the prophetess, the wife of Shallum the son of Tikvah, the son of Harhas, keeper of the wardrobe. (She dwelt in Jerusalem in the Second Quarter.) And they spoke with her. ¹⁵ Then she said to them, "Thus says the Lord God of Israel, 'Tell the man who sent you to Me,

¹⁶ "Thus says the Lord: 'Behold, I will bring calamity on this place and on its inhabitants—all the words of the book which the king of Judah has read— ¹⁷ because they have forsaken Me and burned incense to other gods, that they might provoke Me to anger with all the works of their hands. Therefore My wrath shall be aroused against this place and shall not be quenched.' " ' ¹⁸ But as for the king of Judah, who sent you to inquire of the Lord, in this manner you shall speak to him, 'Thus says the Lord God of Israel: "*Concerning* the words which you have heard— ¹⁹ because your heart was tender, and you humbled yourself before the Lord when you heard what I spoke against this place and against its inhabitants, that they would become a desolation and a curse, and you tore your clothes and wept before Me, I also have heard *you,*" says the Lord. ²⁰ "Surely, therefore, I will gather you to your fathers, and you shall be gathered to your grave in peace; and your eyes shall not see all the calamity which I will bring on this place." ' " So they brought back word to the king.

Phillip's Daughters

Philip the evangelist had four unmarried daughters who were prophets.

Acts 21:7-9
⁷ And when we had finished our voyage from Tyre, we came to Ptolemais, greeted the brethren, and stayed with them one day. ⁸ On the next day we [b]who were Paul's companions departed and came to Caesarea, and entered the house of Philip the evangelist, who was one of the seven, and stayed with him. 9 Now this man had four virgin daughters who prophesied.

The Old Testament prophets were men and women of God who were godly, holy and righteous. People who were ungodly and sinful were terrified when the prophet came to town because that God would show the prophet, and the prophet would expose them. God would use the prophet to rebuke, correct, warn or judge them. The Old Testament prophets received deep revelation from the Lord, and they prophesied with precise detail and accuracy. God is restoring the type of Old Testament prophets today. These present day prophets will have the same anointing that each of these Old Testament prophets had.

Now let's look at some of the better known prophets.

Daniel-The seer (the dreamer and beholder of visions).
The name Daniel means "God is my judge". Daniel was given the Chaldean name Belteshazzar by the commander of the officials of the Babylonian empire when he, along with other Jews, was in captivity. Belteshazzar means "Bel protect the king!" Bel was a Babylonian idol. Isaiah 46:1 describes Bel, an ancient deity- *"Bel bows down, Nebo stoops; Their idols were on the beasts and on the cattle".*

Daniel 1: 1-7
¹ In the third year of the reign of Jehoiakim king of Judah, Nebuchadnezzar king of Babylon came to Jerusalem and besieged it. ² The Lord gave Jehoiakim king of Judah into his hand, along with some of the articles of the house of God; and he brought them into the land of Shinar, to the house of his god, and brought the articles into the treasury of his god. ³ And the [Babylonian] king told Ashpenaz, the chief of his officials, to bring in some of the sons of Israel, including some from the royal family and from

the nobles, ⁴ young men without blemish and handsome in appearance, skillful in all wisdom, endowed with intelligence and discernment, and quick to understand, competent to stand [in the presence of the king] and able to serve in the king's palace. He also ordered Ashpenaz to teach them the literature and language of the Chaldeans. ⁵ The king assigned a daily ration for them from his finest food and from the wine which he drank. They were to be educated and nourished this way for three years so that at the end of that time they were [prepared] to enter the king's service. ⁶ Among them from the sons of Judah were: Daniel, Hananiah, Mishael, and Azariah. ⁷ The commander of the officials gave them [Babylonian] names: Daniel he named Belteshazzar, Hananiah he named Shadrach, Mishael he named Meshach, and Azariah he named Abednego.

Daniel was a young man when he became a Jewish exile living in Babylon. He lived in Babylon throughout the seventy-year captivity of the Jews. He became an administrator over the provincial governors throughout the Babylonian kingdom. Daniel served under 4 kings- Nebuchadnezzar, the Babylonian king; Belshazzar, who reigned in Babylon after the death of his father Nebuchadnezzar; Darius, the king of Persia and Cyrus, also a King of Persia.

Daniel was a seer prophet (a dreamer and beholder of visions). He also had the gift of interpretation of dreams. God gave Daniel great "knowledge and skill in all literature and wisdom; and Daniel had understanding in all visions and dreams" **Daniel 1:16-18**. Daniel interpreted the dreams and vision of Kings Nebuchadnezzar and Belshazzar. He prospered after interpreting the dreams and vison of these kings and was promoted to a high office as result of his faithfulness to God. He was elevated to the positions of political leader, trusted adviser, and reputable prophet.

Nebuchadnezzar's Dream
Daniel 2: 1-13

1 Now in the second year of Nebuchadnezzar's reign, Nebuchadnezzar had dreams; and his spirit was so troubled that his sleep left him. ² Then the king gave the command to call the magicians, the astrologers, the sorcerers, and the Chaldeans to tell the king his dreams. So they came and stood before the king. ³ And the king said to them, "I have had a dream, and my spirit is anxious to [a]know the dream." ⁴ Then the Chaldeans spoke to the king in Aramaic, "O king, live forever! Tell your servants the dream, and we will give the interpretation."⁵ The king answered and said to the Chaldeans, "My [c]decision is firm: if you do not make known the dream to me, and its interpretation, you shall be cut in pieces, and your houses shall be made an ash heap.
⁶ However, if you tell the dream and its interpretation, you shall receive from me gifts, rewards, and great honor. Therefore tell me the dream and its interpretation." ⁷ They answered again and said, "Let the king tell his servants the dream, and we will give its interpretation."⁸ The king answered and said, "I know for certain that you would gain time, because you see that my decision is firm: ⁹ if you do not make known the dream to me, there is only one decree for you! For you have agreed to speak lying and corrupt words before me till the [d]time has changed.

Therefore tell me the dream, and I shall know that you can [e]give me its interpretation." ¹⁰ The Chaldeans answered the king, and said, "There is not a man on earth who can tell the king's matter; therefore no king, lord, or ruler has ever asked such things of any magician, astrologer, or Chaldean. ¹¹ It is a [f]difficult thing that the king requests, and there is no other who can tell it to the king except the gods, whose dwelling is not with flesh." ¹² For this reason the king was angry and very furious and gave the command to destroy all the wise men of Babylon. ¹³ So the decree went out, and they began killing the wise men; and they sought Daniel and his companions, to kill them.

Daniel's Dream Interpretation
Daniel 2: 14-45

¹⁴ Then with counsel and wisdom Daniel answered Arioch, the captain of the king's guard, who had gone out to kill the wise men of Babylon; ¹⁵ he answered and said to Arioch the king's captain, "Why is the decree from the king so [g]urgent?" Then Arioch made the decision known to Daniel. ¹⁶ So Daniel went in and asked the king to give him time, that he might tell the king the interpretation. ¹⁷ Then Daniel went to his house, and made the decision known to Hananiah, Mishael, and Azariah, his companions, ¹⁸ that they might seek mercies from the God of heaven concerning this secret, so that Daniel and his companions might not perish with the rest of the wise men of Babylon. ¹⁹ Then the secret was revealed to Daniel in a night vision. So Daniel blessed the God of heaven. ²⁰ Daniel answered and said: "Blessed be the name of God forever and ever, For wisdom and might are His. ²¹ And He changes the times and the seasons; He removes kings and raises up kings; He gives wisdom to the wise and knowledge to those who have understanding.

²² He reveals deep and secret things; He knows what is in the darkness, And light dwells with Him. ²³ "I thank You and praise You, O God of my fathers; You have given me wisdom and might, And have now made known to me what we asked of You, For You have made known to us the king's [h]demand."²⁴ Therefore Daniel went to Arioch, whom the king had appointed to destroy the wise men of Babylon. He went and said thus to him: "Do not destroy the wise men of Babylon; take me before the king, and I will tell the king the interpretation." ²⁵ Then Arioch quickly brought Daniel before the king, and said thus to him, "I have found a man of the [i]captives of Judah, who will make known to the king the interpretation."²⁶ The king answered and said to Daniel, whose name was Belteshazzar, "Are you able to make known to me the dream which I have seen, and its interpretation?"²⁷ Daniel answered in the presence of the king, and said, "The secret which the king has demanded, the wise men, the astrologers, the magicians, and the soothsayers cannot declare to the king. ²⁸ But there is a God in heaven who reveals secrets, and He has made known to King Nebuchadnezzar what will be in the latter days. Your dream, and the visions of your head upon your bed, were these: ²⁹ As for you, O king, thoughts came to your mind while on your bed, about what would come to pass after this; and He who reveals secrets has made known to you what will be. ³⁰ But as for me, this secret has not been revealed to me because I have more wisdom than anyone living, but for our sakes who make known the interpretation to the king, and that you may [j]know the thoughts of your heart. ³¹ "You, O king, were watching; and behold, a great image! This great image, whose splendor was excellent, stood before you; and its form was awesome. ³² This image's head was of fine gold, its chest and arms of silver, its belly and [k]thighs of bronze, ³³ its legs of iron, its feet partly of iron and partly of [l]clay. 34 You

watched while a stone was cut out without hands, which struck the image on its feet of iron and clay, and broke them in pieces. ³⁵ Then the iron, the clay, the bronze, the silver, and the gold were crushed together, and became like chaff from the summer threshing floors; the wind carried them away so that no trace of them was found. And the stone that struck the image became a great mountain and filled the whole earth.³⁶ "This is the dream. Now we will tell the interpretation of it before the king. ³⁷ You, O king, are a king of kings. For the God of heaven has given you a kingdom, power, strength, and glory; ³⁸ and wherever the children of men dwell, or the beasts of the field and the birds of the heaven, He has given them into your hand, and has made you ruler over them all—you are this head of gold. ³⁹ But after you shall arise another kingdom inferior to yours; then another, a third kingdom of bronze, which shall rule over all the earth. ⁴⁰ And the fourth kingdom shall be as strong as iron, inasmuch as iron breaks in pieces and shatters everything; and like iron that crushes, that kingdom will break in pieces and crush all the others. ⁴¹ Whereas you saw the feet and toes, partly of potter's clay and partly of iron, the kingdom shall be divided; yet the strength of the iron shall be in it, just as you saw the iron mixed with ceramic clay. ⁴² And as the toes of the feet were partly of iron and partly of clay, so the kingdom shall be partly strong and partly [m]fragile. ⁴³ As you saw iron mixed with ceramic clay, they will mingle with the seed of men; but they will not adhere to one another, just as iron does not mix with clay. ⁴⁴ And in the days of these kings the God of heaven will set up a kingdom which shall never be destroyed; and the kingdom shall not be left to other people; it shall [n]break in pieces and [o]consume all these kingdoms, and it shall stand forever. ⁴⁵ Inasmuch as you saw that the stone was cut out of the mountain without hands, and that it broke in pieces the iron, the bronze, the clay, the silver, and the gold—the great God has made known to the king what will come to pass after this. The dream is certain, and its interpretation is sure."

Daniel's Promotion
Daniel 2: 46-48

[46] Then King Nebuchadnezzar fell on his face, prostrate before Daniel, and commanded that they should present an offering and incense to him. [47] The king answered Daniel, and said, "Truly your God *is* the God of gods, the Lord of kings, and a revealer of secrets, since you could reveal this secret." [48] Then the king promoted Daniel and gave him many great gifts; and he made him ruler over the whole province of Babylon, and chief administrator over all the wise *men* of Babylon. [49] Also Daniel petitioned the king, and he set Shadrach, Meshach, and Abed-Nego over the affairs of the province of Babylon; but **Daniel *sat* in the gate of the king.**

Darius's Vision
Daniel 5:1-12

[1] Belshazzar the king made a great feast for a thousand of his lords, and drank wine in the presence of the thousand. [2] While he tasted the wine, Belshazzar gave the command to bring the gold and silver vessels which his father Nebuchadnezzar had taken from the temple which *had been* in Jerusalem, that the king and his lords, his wives, and his concubines might drink from them. [3] Then they brought the gold vessels that had been taken from the temple of the house of God which *had been* in Jerusalem; and the king and his lords, his wives, and his concubines drank from them. [4] They drank wine, and praised the gods of gold and silver, bronze and iron, wood and stone.

⁵ In the same hour the fingers of a man's hand appeared and wrote opposite the lampstand on the plaster of the wall of the king's palace; and the king saw the part of the hand that wrote. ⁶ Then the king's countenance changed, and his thoughts troubled him, so that the joints of his hips were loosened and his knees knocked against each other. ⁷ The king cried aloud to bring in the astrologers, the Chaldeans, and the soothsayers. The king spoke, saying to the wise *men* of Babylon, "Whoever reads this writing, and tells me its interpretation, shall be clothed with purple and *have* a chain of gold around his neck; and he shall be the third ruler in the kingdom." ⁸ Now all the king's wise *men* came, but they could not read the writing, or make known to the king its interpretation. ⁹ Then King Belshazzar was greatly troubled, his countenance was changed, and his lords were [astonished. ¹⁰ The queen, because of the words of the king and his lords, came to the banquet hall. The queen spoke, saying, "O king, live forever! Do not let your thoughts trouble you, nor let your countenance change. ¹¹ There is a man in your kingdom in whom *is* the Spirit of the Holy God. And in the days of your father, light and understanding and wisdom, like the wisdom of the gods, were found in him; and King Nebuchadnezzar your father—your father the king—made him chief of the magicians, astrologers, Chaldeans, *and* soothsayers. ¹² Inasmuch as an excellent spirit, knowledge, understanding, interpreting dreams, solving riddles, and explaining enigmas were found in this Daniel, whom the king named Belteshazzar, now let Daniel be called, and he will give the interpretation."

Daniel's Interpretation of Darius's Vision
Daniel 5:13-28

¹³ Then Daniel was brought in before the king. The king spoke, and said to Daniel, "*Are* you that Daniel who is one of the captives from Judah, whom my ʲfather the king brought from Judah? ¹⁴ I have heard of you, that the Spirit of God *is* in you, and *that* light and understanding and excellent wisdom are found in you. ¹⁵ Now the wise *men,* the astrologers, have been brought in before me, that they should read this writing and make known to me its interpretation, but they could not give the interpretation of the thing. ¹⁶ And I have heard of you, that you can give interpretations and explain enigmas. Now if you can read the writing and make known to me its interpretation, you shall be clothed with purple and *have* a chain of gold around your neck, and shall be the third ruler in the kingdom." ¹⁷ Then Daniel answered, and said before the king, "Let your gifts be for yourself, and give your rewards to another; yet I will read the writing to the king, and make known to him the interpretation. ¹⁸ O king, the Most High God gave Nebuchadnezzar your father a kingdom and majesty, glory and honor. ¹⁹ And because of the majesty that He gave him, all peoples, nations, and languages trembled and feared before him. Whomever he wished, he executed; whomever he wished, he kept alive; whomever he wished, he set up; and whomever he wished, he put down. ²⁰ But when his heart was lifted up, and his spirit was hardened in pride, he was deposed from his kingly throne, and they took his glory from him. ²¹ Then he was driven from the sons of men, his heart was made like the beasts, and his dwelling *was* with the wild donkeys. They fed him with grass like oxen, and his body was wet with the dew of heaven, till he knew that the Most High God rules in the kingdom of men, and appoints over it whomever He chooses.²² "But you his son, Belshazzar, have not humbled

your heart, although you knew all this. ²³ And you have lifted yourself up against the Lord of heaven. They have brought the vessels of His house before you, and you and your lords, your wives and your concubines, have drunk wine from them. And you have praised the gods of silver and gold, bronze and iron, wood and stone, which do not see or hear or know; and the God who holds your breath in His hand and owns all your ways, you have not glorified. ²⁴ Then the fingers of the hand were sent from Him, and this writing was written. ²⁵ "And this is the inscription that was written:
MENE,MENE, TEKEL, UPHARSIN.
²⁶ This is the interpretation of each word. MENE: God has numbered your kingdom, and finished it; ²⁷ TEKEL: You have been weighed in the balances, and found wanting; ²⁸ PERES: Your kingdom has been divided, and given to the Medes and Persians."

Daniel's Promotion
Daniel 5:29
²⁹ Then Belshazzar gave the command, and they clothed Daniel with purple and *put* a chain of gold around his neck, and made a proclamation concerning him that he should be the third ruler in the kingdom.

Daniel also had many prophetic visions from the Lord. These prophetic visions were given to Daniel from 605 - 535 BC.
Daniel 7. Daniel 10.

Anna – prophet, worshipper, intercessor and evangelist.
The name Anna means grace. Anna, the prophetess, was the daughter of Phanuel. She belonged to the tribe of Asher, one

of the least tribes of Israel. Anna was a virgin when she married her husband. Her husband died just seven years after their marriage. From that time onwards, Anna devoted her life to prayer and fasting. She "*did not depart from the temple, but served God with fastings and prayers night and day*" Luke 2: 37.

Anna was in the temple when Joseph and Mary brought the young Jesus to Jerusalem to present Him to the Lord and to offer a sacrifice according to the law of the Lord. Simeon, a just and devout Jew was in the temple at the time because the Holy Spirit revealed to him that he would not die before he had seen the Lord Jesus Christ. When he saw Jesus in the temple with Joseph and Mary, held Him in his arms and blessed God that He lived to see the Savior of the world.

Anna, who was eighty-four years at the time, witnessed the memorable event. She entered the temple at the precise moment that Simeon praised the Lord for letting him see the Messiah before he died. As a prophet she knew that the Child Jesus was the promised Messiah sent to redeem mankind from their sins. The instant she saw Jesus, she worshipped the Lord and "*spoke of Him to all those who looked for redemption in Jerusalem*". Luke 22: 38. God used Anna as an evangelist to spread the gospel of Jesus Christ to many people. Anna's ministry was that of prophet, worshipper, intercessor and evangelist.

Luke 22: 36-38
[36] Now there was one, Anna, a prophetess, the daughter of Phanuel, of the tribe of Asher.

She was of a great age, and had lived with a husband seven years from her virginity; ³⁷ and this woman *was* a widow of about eighty-four years, who did not depart from the temple, but served *God* with fastings and prayers night and day. ³⁸ And coming in that instant she gave thanks to [¹]the Lord, and spoke of Him to all those who looked for redemption in Jerusalem.

Jeremiah-
The weeping prophet and a prophet of warning and judgment.

God called Jeremiah to be a prophet when he was very young. But Jeremiah struggled with the call. He protested and told the Lord, "I do not know how to speak, for I am only a youth" Jeremiah 1: 6. The Lord assured Jeremiah that he would put his own words in Jeremiah's mouth and make him a prophet to the nations.

Jeremiah 1: 4-10
⁴ Then the word of the Lord came to me, saying:⁵ "Before I formed you in the womb I knew you; Before you were born I sanctified[you; I ordained you a prophet to the nations."⁶ Then said I:"Ah, Lord God!
Behold, I cannot speak, for I *am* a youth."
⁷ But the Lord said to me:
"Do not say, 'I *am* a youth,'
For you shall go to all to whom I send you,
And whatever I command you, you shall speak.
⁸ Do not be afraid of their faces,
For I *am* with you to deliver you," says the Lord.
⁹ Then the Lord put forth His hand and touched my mouth, and the Lord said to me:

"Behold, I have put My words in your mouth.
¹⁰ See, I have this day set you over the nations and over the kingdoms, To root out and to pull down, To destroy and to throw down, To build and to plant."

Jeremiah prophesied against Israel's false worship and idolatry, and urged them to repent. But they refused to repent. He also warned Israel to stay in Judah. But they refused.

Jeremiah 42: 7-22
⁷ And it happened after ten days that the word of the Lord came to Jeremiah. ⁸ Then he called Johanan the son of Kareah, all the captains of the forces which *were* with him, and all the people from the least even to the greatest, ⁹ and said to them, "Thus says the Lord, the God of Israel, to whom you sent me to present your petition before Him: ¹⁰ 'If you will still remain in this land, then I will build you and not pull *you* down, and I will plant you and not pluck *you* up. For I relent concerning the disaster that I have brought upon you. ¹¹ Do not be afraid of the king of Babylon, of whom you are afraid; do not be afraid of him,' says the Lord, 'for I *am* with you, to save you and deliver you from his hand. ¹² And I will show you mercy, that he may have mercy on you and cause you to return to your own land.' ¹³ "But if you say, 'We will not dwell in this land,' disobeying the voice of the Lord your God, ¹⁴ saying, 'No, but we will go to the land of Egypt where we shall see no war, nor hear the sound of the trumpet, nor be hungry for bread, and there we will dwell'— ¹⁵ Then hear now the word of the Lord, O remnant of Judah! Thus says the Lord of hosts, the God of Israel: 'If you wholly set your faces to enter Egypt, and go to dwell there, ¹⁶ then it shall be *that* the sword which you

feared shall overtake you there in the land of Egypt; the famine of which you were afraid shall follow close after you there in Egypt; and there you shall die. [17] So shall it be with all the men who set their faces to go to Egypt to dwell there. They shall die by the sword, by famine, and by pestilence. And none of them shall remain or escape from the disaster that I will bring upon them.' [18] "For thus says the Lord of hosts, the God of Israel: 'As My anger and My fury have been poured out on the inhabitants of Jerusalem, so will My fury be poured out on you when you enter Egypt. And you shall be an oath, an astonishment, a curse, and a reproach; and you shall see this place no more.' [19] "The Lord has said concerning you, O remnant of Judah, 'Do not go to Egypt!' Know certainly that I have admonished you this day. [20] For you were hypocrites in your hearts when you sent me to the Lord your God, saying, 'Pray for us to the Lord our God, and according to all that the Lord your God says, so declare to us and we will do it.' [21] And I have this day declared it to you, but you have not obeyed the voice of the Lord your God, or anything which He has sent you by me. [22] Now therefore, know certainly that you shall die by the sword, by famine, and by pestilence in the place where you desire to go to dwell."

God had commanded Jeremiah to prophesy warning, judgment and correction to Israel, but He told him they would not listen.

Jeremiah 7:27
[27] "Therefore you shall speak all these words to them, but they will not obey you. You shall also call to them, but they will not answer you.

Jeremiah obeyed God, knowing Israel would not listen and suffered tremendously for the prophecies he released. He was beaten and put in the stocks (Jeremiah 20:1-2). He was sentenced to death (Jeremiah 26:11) He was left to die in the mud (Jeremiah 38:6). He was called a liar (Jeremiah 43:2).

David the prophetic psalmist
David was a great warrior, a worshipper, a prophet, a shepherd, a man of integrity and a man after God's own. Heart. He was greatest King of Israel and Judah. Although God chose, ordained and anointed David as King after Saul sinned against God and had to be replaced as King, it took years before David was actually recognized as King and placed in the palace.

David was constantly on the run from Saul, hiding in caves and dens. He was greatly persecuted and despised by Saul. Saul was jealous of him because of his character, and tried to kill David many times. David thought he would be installed as King right after Samuel anointed him, but he experienced years of suffering and persecution before he could actually become king.

David loved the Lord wholeheartedly. He worshipped and praised the Lord with all his might. He didn't care what anyone thought about him. He didn't care if they mocked him or ridiculed him. He was a radical worshipper. His excellent character reflected that all he said and did was an act of worship unto the Lord. He loved the Lord with all His heart. In fact, the name David means loving.

When David was installed as King, he reinstated true worship unto God. David desired to have continual praise and worship offered up to the Lord – true worship that ushered in the glory of God; worship that exalted the Lord; worship that magnified Him; worship that pleased Him. He pitched a tabernacle to house the Ark of God and placed it in the center of it. And he appointed Levites *(the Levites were priests)* as singers and musicians to minister before the Ark. He rebuilt and restored the Tabernacle of worship which had been broken down and established a new worship order led by four thousand prophetic singers and musicians who ministered to God as their full time job. They never stopped praising and worshipping God 24/7. According to history, this went on for 36 years. David penned most of the psalms which were prophetic.

Question:
Which type of prophet described in this chapter are you? Why?

_____

_____

_____

_____

_____

_____

_____

_____

_____

_____

_____

_____

Chapter 11
Jezebel: The Destroyer of Prophets

Jezebel was an evil woman who became queen when she married Ahab, the King of Israel. She was the daughter of Ethbaal, the king of the Sidonians, and the high priest of Baal, an evil deity. The worship of Baal involved human sacrifice and ritual temple prostitution. Baal worshippers engaged in deviant sensuality and lewd and perverted sex acts. Jezebel, as a priestess of Baal was raised in this environment where sex was used to gain power. Ahab was a weak and passive King who was completely manipulated and dominated by Jezebel.

1 Kings 16:31-32 Amplified
[31] It came about, as if it had been a trivial thing for Ahab to walk in the sins of Jeroboam the son of Nebat, that he married Jezebel the daughter of Ethbaal king of the Sidonians, and went and served Baal and worshiped him. [32] So he erected an altar for Baal in the house of Baal which he built in Samaria.

When Jezebel married Ahab, she introduced Baal worship and the worship of Ashtoreth to Israel. Ashtoreth is a goddess of love, sexual perversion and sensuality. She was believed to be a consort (the spouse of a reigning monarch) of Baal. Ashtoreth's priestesses and temple prostitutes lured and engaged in sexual intercourse with the men of Israel. It is estimated that Jezebel swayed 10 million Israelites into leaving the worship of God for Baal and Ashtoreth . (Hamilton, 2013)

Elijah, the prophet of the Lord, confronts the prophets of Baal on Mount Carmel.

Elijah had a major victory on Mount Carmel when he challenged the prophets of Baal to prove that Jehovah God is the only true God and that their gods were weak and useless idols.

1 Kings 18:20-40
[20] So Ahab sent for all the children of Israel, and gathered the prophets together on Mount Carmel.
[21] And Elijah came to all the people, and said, "How long will you falter between two opinions? If the Lord *is* God, follow Him; but if Baal, follow him." But the people answered him not a word. [22] Then Elijah said to the people, "I alone am left a prophet of the Lord; but Baal's prophets *are* four hundred and fifty men. [23] Therefore let them give us two bulls; and let them choose one bull for themselves, cut it in pieces, and lay *it* on the wood, but put no fire *under it*; and I will prepare the other bull, and lay *it* on the wood, but put no fire *under it.* [24] Then you call on the name of your gods, and I will call

on the name of the Lord; and the God who answers by fire, He is God."So all the people answered and said, [e]"It is well spoken."²⁵ Now Elijah said to the prophets of Baal, "Choose one bull for yourselves and prepare *it* first, for you *are* many; and call on the name of your god, but put no fire *under it.*"

²⁶ So they took the bull which was given them, and they prepared *it,* and called on the name of Baal from morning even till noon, saying, "O Baal, [f]hear us!" But *there was* no voice; no one answered. Then they [g]leaped about the altar which they had made. ²⁷ And so it was, at noon, that Elijah mocked them and said, "Cry [h]aloud, for he *is* a god; either he is meditating, or he is busy, or he is on a journey, *or* perhaps he is sleeping and must be awakened." ²⁸ So they cried aloud, and cut themselves, as was their custom, with [i]knives and lances, until the blood gushed out on them. ²⁹ And when midday was past, they prophesied until the *time* of the offering of the *evening* sacrifice. But *there was* no voice; no one answered, no one paid attention.³⁰ Then Elijah said to all the people, "Come near to me." So all the people came near to him. And he repaired the altar of the Lord *that was* broken down. ³¹ And Elijah took twelve stones, according to the number of the tribes of the sons of Jacob, to whom the word of the Lord had come, saying, "Israel shall be your name." ³² Then with the stones he built an altar in the name of the Lord; and he made a trench around the altar large enough to hold two seahs of seed.³³ And he put the wood in order, cut the bull in pieces, and laid *it* on the wood, and said, "Fill four waterpots with water, and pour *it* on the burnt sacrifice and on the wood." ³⁴ Then he said, "Do *it* a second time," and they did *it* a second time; and he said, "Do *it* a third time," and they did *it* a third time.

⁳⁵ So the water ran all around the altar; and he also filled the trench with water.³⁶ And it came to pass, at *the time of* the offering of the *evening* sacrifice, that Elijah the prophet came near and said, "Lord God of Abraham, Isaac, and Israel, let it be known this day that You *are* God in Israel and I *am* Your servant, and *that* I have done all these things at Your word. ³⁷ Hear me, O Lord, hear me, that this people may know that You *are* the Lord God, and *that* You have turned their hearts back *to You* again." ³⁸ Then the fire of the Lord fell and consumed the burnt sacrifice, and the wood and the stones and the dust, and it licked up the water that *was* in the trench. ³⁹ Now when all the people saw *it,* they fell on their faces; and they said, "The Lord, He *is* God! The Lord, He *is* God!"⁴⁰ And Elijah said to them, "Seize the prophets of Baal! Do not let one of them escape!" So they seized them; and Elijah brought them down to the Brook Kishon and executed them there.

When Jezebel heard of the incident, she threatened to kill Elijah. After the major victory on Mt. Carmel, Elijah became fearful and ran for his life from Jezebel.

1 Kings 19:1-3 AMP
[1] Now Ahab told Jezebel all that Elijah had done, and how he had killed all the prophets [of Baal] with the sword. [2] Then Jezebel sent a messenger to Elijah, saying, "So may the gods do to me, and even more, if by this time tomorrow I do not make your life like the life of one of them." [3] And Elijah was afraid and arose and ran for his life, and he came to Beersheba which belongs to Judah, and he left his servant there.

Elijah hid from Jezebel. Such was Jezebel's evil power that Elijah became depressed and no longer wanted to be a prophet. God eventually passed the prophetic mantle to Elisha. Elisha became the prophet in place of Elijah.

1 Kings 19:9-16 AMP
[9] There he came to a cave and spent the night in it; and behold, the word of the LORD came to him, and He said to him, "What are you doing here, Elijah?" [10] He said, "I have been very zealous (impassioned) for the LORD God of hosts (armies) [proclaiming what is rightfully and uniquely His]; for the sons of Israel have abandoned (broken) Your covenant, torn down Your altars, and killed Your prophets with the sword. And I, only I, am left; and they seek to take away my life." [11] So He said, "Go out and stand on the mountain before the LORD." And behold, the LORD was passing by, and a great and powerful wind was tearing out the mountains and breaking the rocks in pieces before the LORD; but the LORD was not in the wind. And after the wind, [there was] an earthquake, but the LORD was not in the earthquake. [12] After the earthquake, [there was] a fire, but the LORD was not in the fire; and after the fire, [there was] the sound of a gentle blowing. [13] When Elijah heard the sound, he wrapped his face in his mantle (cloak) and went out and stood in the entrance of the cave. And behold, a voice came to him and said, "What are you doing here, Elijah?" [14] He said, "I have been very zealous for the LORD God of hosts (armies), because the sons of Israel have abandoned (broken) Your covenant, torn down Your altars and killed Your prophets with the sword. And I, only I, am left; and they seek to take away my life." [15] The LORD said to him, "Go, return on your way to the Wilderness

of Damascus; and when you arrive, you shall anoint Hazael as king over Aram (Syria); [16] and you shall anoint Jehu the son of Nimshi as king over Israel; and anoint Elisha the son of Shaphat of Abel-meholah as prophet in your place.

The Spirit of Jezebel

Jezebel is dead. But the spirit of Jezebel is still terrorizing people today. The spirit of Jezebel is an ancient spirit that existed long before Jezebel was born. The Jezebel spirit is a destroyer of prophets. It opposes the prophetic. We are not to tolerate Jezebel. The Lord gave this warning to the Church:

Revelation 2:18-23 AMP

[18] "And to the angel (divine messenger) of the church in Thyatira write: "These are the words of the Son of God, who has eyes [that flash] like a flame of fire [in righteous judgment], and whose feet are like burnished [white-hot] bronze: [19] 'I know your deeds, your love and faith and service and patient endurance, and that your last deeds are more numerous and greater than the first. [20] But I have this [charge] against you, that you tolerate the woman Jezebel, who calls herself a prophetess [claiming to be inspired], and she teaches and misleads My bond-servants so that they commit [acts of sexual] immorality and eat food sacrificed to idols. [21] I gave her time to repent [to change her inner self and her sinful way of thinking], but she has no desire to repent of her immorality and refuses to do so. [22] Listen carefully, I will throw her on a bed of sickness, and those who commit adultery with her [I will bring] into great anguish, unless they repent of her deeds. [23] And I will kill her children (followers) with pestilence [thoroughly annihilating them], and all the churches will know [without any doubt] that I am

He who searches the minds and hearts [the innermost thoughts, purposes]; and I will give to each one of you [a reward or punishment] according to your deeds.

Jezebel's Mission

The word Jezebel means cannot cohabitate. Jezebel cannot live with anyone she cannot control or dominate. The Jezebel spirit is a highly combative and confrontational spirit that demands having its own way all the time. Jezebel will often appear to be submissive, but it is a cunning plot to gain power and influence over its subject. Jezebel's submissiveness is false. Do not be deceived by it. It is a clever ploy she uses to seek to be in control at all times.

People with a Jezebel spirit appear to be deeply spiritual and prophetic, but it is a deception. Jezebel "calls herself a prophetess (Revelation 2:18-23) " and often manipulates others with her " prophecies". She believes that her prophetic voice is more accurate and superior to all other prophetic voices.

A person with a Jezebel spirit very quickly forms a close bond with apostles and prophets. She does this so she can control, manipulate, influence them and gain their confidence. The spirit of Jezebel has a deep hatred of prophets and true spiritual authority. Jezebel uses emotional manipulation , witchcraft, seduction and flattery to gain control and power over her subjects. She does this subtly and gradually so that her subjects won't easily discern who she really is and what her evil intent is. Jezebel's end game is to destroy true prophets of God and replace them with false prophets.

Jezebel causes demonic depression and loss of vision. Jezebel robs you of your joy. With just a single threat from Jezebel, Elijah became afraid and fled into the wilderness. He became depressed and lost his vision regarding his ministry. He even begged the Lord to kill him.

> **1 Kings 19:4 AMP**
> [4] But he himself traveled a day's journey into the wilderness, and he came and sat down under a juniper tree and asked [God] that he might die. He said, "It is enough; now, O LORD, take my life, for I am no better than my fathers."

"Jezebel intimidates through fear, threats and witchcraft and causes prophets to quit and want to die. Jezebel thrives on attention. She desires to be the focus of attention at all times. Jezebel gets inside your mind and consumes your thoughts until all you think about is her. She makes you feel guilty, and that something is wrong with you, even though you have done nothing wrong. Those under attack may awaken one morning to find it takes effort just to breathe. All joy seems to depart. Spiritual life seems irrelevant. Demonic voices will echo in their minds "something's wrong with you!" They may suddenly find themselves in unreasonable anxiety, fearing tragedy or death. Much of what is called "depression" in the ministry is simply Jezebel!" (Henson, 2009)

How to Identify the spirit of Jezebel

You must have spiritual discernment to identify the spirit of Jezebel. The Jezebel spirit usually manifests in women, but sometimes also manifests in men.

The following excerpt is taken from the article "What is Jezebel Spirit and How it Operates by Michael Bradley".

What is Jezebel Spirit and How it Operates.
By: Michael Bradley
(Source: http://www.bible-knowledge.com/the-jezebel-spirit-and-how-it-operates/

1. The Jezebel Spirit Is Under The Influence Of Witchcraft.

Anyone in the church, especially operating under the influence of witchcraft is a Jezebel (2 Kings 9:22). Not only will she use witchcraft, but she will also use control, manipulation, sex, religion, rumor spreading, gossip, and false prophecies.

2. Jezebel Spirits Promote Seduction And Sexual Immorality.

The Jezebel spirit uses sex to move people away from God. Some of the most seemingly spiritual women in the church have a spirit of whoredom and are used by Satan to seduce men from their godly stance (Revelation 2:20-21). They are usually sexually unclean. They will use sexual seduction combined with a false spirituality to lure men into sin (2 Kings 9:30). Beware of anyone who seems spiritual but is willing to sin sexually. Sex brings oneness with a person. Therefore, her spirits can transfer.

3. Jezebel Operates In False Prophecy. (Revelation 2:20)

They push themselves off as prophets because if they say that God is giving the message, then it forces people to hear them. They are attracted to strong prophetic, charismatic churches where they can easily sow their false prophecies.

4. Jezebel Uses Titles To Give Herself Influence.

Beware of those who use self-proclaimed titles or call themselves prophets, without these titles being bestowed upon them by church authority.

5. Jezebel Spirits Can Look The Part Spiritually.

Jezebel spirits have the ability to work through some of the sweetest-looking, nicest, most spiritual people you ever see in your life. They are usually gifted, loyal, self-sacrificing, giving, praying people. But in most cases there is an open wound or character flaw that was never confronted or healed that Satan attaches himself to, in order to work through. They can praise God, talk the lingo, and pray in tongues. They are very super-spiritual and tend to come off as super flakes with their own super revelation, and they end up being a super hassle to a pastor. They appear to be really deep, deeper than God and the pastor.

6. Jezebels Look For Authority Without Much Responsibility.

They don't care about fulfilling the responsibilities of their position.

7. Jezebel Spirits Work To Get Close To Leadership.

Before the people (at least outwardly), the pastor can do no wrong. She always suggests what should be done for the pastor. She promotes the pastor in front of everyone. She is always available when the pastor needs someone. She gives him and his family special gifts. She always flatters the pastor, always has a word for him, and always tries to encourage him in order to win his confidence so she can push her agenda.

8. Jezebel Spirits Want To Be In Leadership And Usually Achieve It.

In leadership, Jezebels have influence with the pastor's approval. People follow her because they think she is sanctioned by the pastor. She usually gets into leadership and begins to sow seeds of discord and false teaching into the minds of the people to lead them astray from the pastor's authority. Most pastors end up placing women like this in leadership because they need help from people whom they perceive to have some maturity. But time reveals that Jezebel spirits ultimately challenge the pastor's teachings, causing people to question and doubt his leadership.

9. Jezebel Spirits Will Start Their Own Following.

They thrive on people's affirmation and attention. They usually attract to them other wounded women who have been rejected and who are dysfunctional. She has her own cultic following and will usually influence women to leave their marriages so she can rule them. They think that she has spiritual strength as a woman and want to be like her.

10. Jezebel Hates Male Authority, Especially True Men Of God.

Just as Jezebel hated Elijah the prophet of God, that spirit hates true men of God today who walk in their authority (1 Kings 19:1-2). Although they may act outwardly as if they are with the pastor, inwardly, they are working to tear his ministry down. If, for some reason, they cannot get through to the senior pastor, they will try to work through his assistant or associate leaders. She puts her and her prophecies above leadership. Her doctrine is divisive. She uses her prophecies to give out words such as, "Divorce him," "Leave the church," "Give me your tithe," or "It won't be blessed unless you put it in my hand." "Speak to me only. Don't go to anyone else."

11. Jezebel Acts Like She Really Cares About The Pastor.

Jezebel acts as if she cares about the pastor and wants to pray for him and his wife. But she uses this as a false spiritual tactic to spread her gossip. She will pray "Please, God, show our pastor the revelation and things you have shown us. Open his eyes that he may see that this is the way. Lead him into deeper truth like you have given us." Then people begin to think that the pastor is not deep enough and that they need to go to another church. Now she accomplishes her assignment of pulling people away from their church.

12. Jezebels Usually Have Husbands Whom They Can Dominate.

Just as Jezebel had a weak-spine husband in Ahab, domineering women will usually find men they can rule or who will let them have their way. She will make sure she wears the pants.

13. Jezebels Want Places Of Greatest Influence Over People.

Why? The more people she can lay her hands on, pray for, or prophesy to, the more people she can connect her spirits to. Everyone she touches now has a spiritual tentacle tied to her.

14. Jezebels Want To Kill True Prophets Of God.

Why? True prophets will expose them and hinder their agenda against a church. She will try to use her witchcraft to either bring an early death or kill his reputation. True prophets of God who have the Shamar anointing have the ability to keep the Jezebel spirit out (Hosea 12:13).

15. Jezebel Spirits Come To Destroy A Man Of God's Calling.

Jezebel's witchcraft was so strong that she caused Elijah to be suicidal right after his greatest victory for God (1 Kings 19:3-4). Jezebel wants pastors to quit, run, leave town, leave the ministry, divorce their wives, and give up. When pastors are sensing that, most likely someone is performing witchcraft behind the scenes.

16. Jezebels Will Use Divide-And-Conquer Tactics.

Satan (the serpent) lured Eve away from her husband's authority, which opened the door for him to conquer them. He uses the same strategy today. Jezebels get close to the pastor and his wife. They work to isolate, split, and divide the man and the woman. They go to work on the weaker vessel first, pouring their poison into the wife's mind and dividing her from her husband. Then she will work to either get him for herself or sway him to get involved in sexual immorality because his wife is no longer present emotionally.

Every church that moves into the things of God, especially things of the Spirit such as speaking in tongues, prophecy, spiritual gifts, praise and worship, casting out demons, laying on of hands and healing, will become a target for witchcraft and the Jezebel spirit. Any church that hits Satan's radar and becomes a threat to the kingdom of darkness will see an infiltration of the Jezebel spirit.

Churches that reject the supernatural power of God become increasingly irrelevant and unable to reach the world, for the battle for men's souls is intensely supernatural in nature.For all who operate in witchcraft or in a Jezebel spirit, the Word of God reveals their end. The Word of God states that the ultimate end of a witch is death. Thou shalt not suffer a witch to live (Exodus 22:18).

Many people erroneously believe that it was the Elijah who defeated Jezebel. It was Jehu and not Elijah who defeated Jezebel.

2 Kings 9

¹ And Elisha the prophet called one of the sons of the prophets, and said to him, "Get[a] yourself ready, take this flask of oil in your hand, and go to Ramoth Gilead. ² Now when you arrive at that place, look there for Jehu the son of Jehoshaphat, the son of Nimshi, and go in and make him rise up from among his associates, and take him to an inner room. ³ Then take the flask of oil, and pour *it* on his head, and say, 'Thus says the Lord: "I have anointed you king over Israel."
Then open the door and flee, and do not delay."⁴ So the young man, the servant of the prophet, went to Ramoth Gilead. ⁵ And when he arrived, there *were* the captains of the army sitting; and he said, "I have a message for you, Commander. "Jehu said, For which *one* of us?"

"And he said, "For you, Commander." ⁶ Then he arose and went into the house. And he poured the oil on his head, and said to him, "Thus says the Lord God of Israel: 'I have anointed you king over the people of the Lord, over Israel. ⁷ You shall strike down the house of Ahab your master, that I may avenge the blood of My servants the prophets, and the blood of all the servants of the Lord, at the hand of Jezebel. ⁸ For the whole house of Ahab shall perish; and I will cut off from Ahab all the males in Israel, both bond and free. ⁹ So I will make the house of Ahab like the house of Jeroboam the son of Nebat, and like the house of Baasha the son of Ahijah. ¹⁰ The dogs shall eat Jezebel on the plot *of ground* at Jezreel, and *there shall be* none to bury *her*.' " And he opened the door and fled.¹¹ Then Jehu came out to the servants of his master, and *one* said to him, "*Is* all well? Why did this madman come to you?"And he said to them, "You know the man and his babble."¹² And they said, "A lie! Tell us now." So he said, "Thus and thus he spoke to me, saying, 'Thus says the Lord: "I have anointed you king over Israel." ' "¹³ Then each man hastened to take his garment and put *it* [b]under him on the top of the steps; and they blew trumpets, saying, "Jehu is king!"¹⁴ So Jehu the son of Jehoshaphat, the son of Nimshi, conspired against Joram. (Now Joram had been defending Ramoth Gilead, he and all Israel, against Hazael king of Syria. ¹⁵ But King [c]Joram had returned to Jezreel to recover from the wounds which the Syrians had inflicted on him when he fought with Hazael king of Syria.) And Jehu said, "If you are so minded, let no one leave *or* escape from the city to go and tell *it* in Jezreel." ¹⁶ So Jehu rode in a chariot and went to Jezreel, for Joram was laid up there; and Ahaziah king of Judah had come down to see Joram.¹⁷ Now a watchman stood on the tower in Jezreel, and he saw the company of Jehu as he came, and said, "I see a company of men." And Joram said, "Get a horseman and send him to meet them, and let him say, [d]'*Is it* peace?' "¹⁸ So the horseman went to meet him, and said, "Thus says the king: '*Is it* peace?' "And Jehu said,

"What have you to do with peace? Turn around and follow me. "So the watchman reported, saying, "The messenger went to them, but is not coming back."¹⁹ Then he sent out a second horseman who came to them, and said, "Thus says the king: '*Is it* peace?' "And Jehu answered, "What have you to do with peace? Turn around and follow me."²⁰ So the watchman reported, saying, "He went up to them and is not coming back; and the driving *is* like the driving of Jehu the son of Nimshi, for he drives furiously!"²¹ Then Joram said, []"Make ready." And his chariot was made ready. Then Joram king of Israel and Ahaziah king of Judah went out, each in his chariot; and they went out to meet Jehu, and met him on the property of Naboth the Jezreelite. ²² Now it happened, when Joram saw Jehu, that he said, "*Is it* peace, Jehu? So he answered, "What peace, as long as the harlotries of your mother Jezebel and her witchcraft *are so* many? ³⁰ Now when Jehu had come to Jezreel, Jezebel heard of it; and she put paint on her eyes and adorned her head, and looked through a window. ³¹ Then, as Jehu entered at the gate, she said, "Is it peace, Zimri, murderer of your master?"³² And he looked up at the window, and said, "Who is on my side? Who?" So two or three eunuchs looked out at him. ³³ Then he said, "Throw her down." So they threw her down, and some of her blood spattered on the wall and on the horses; and he trampled her underfoot. ³⁴ And when he had gone in, he ate and drank. Then he said, "Go now, see to this accursed woman, and bury her, for she was a king's daughter." ³⁵ So they went to bury her, but they found no more of her than the skull and the feet and the palms of her hands. ³⁶ Therefore they came back and told him. And he said, "This is the word of the Lord, which He spoke by His servant Elijah the Tishbite, saying, 'On the plot of ground at Jezreel dogs shall eat the flesh of Jezebel; ³⁷ and the corpse of Jezebel shall be as refuse on the surface of the field, in the plot at Jezreel, so that they shall not say, "Here lies Jezebel."

Chapter 12
Myths regarding prophets and prophecies

Myth
You should not ask a prophet for a prophetic word.

Truth
It is ok to inquire of a prophet.

> **1 Kings 22: 1-9**
> Now three years passed without war between Syria and Israel. ² Then it came to pass, in the third year, that Jehoshaphat the king of Judah went down to *visit* the king of Israel.³ And the king of Israel said to his servants, "Do you know that Ramoth in Gilead *is* ours, but we hesitate to take it out of the hand of the king of Syria?" ⁴ So he said to Jehoshaphat, "Will you go with me to fight at Ramoth Gilead? "Jehoshaphat said to the king of Israel, "I *am* as you *are,* my people as your people, my horses as your horses." ⁵ Also Jehoshaphat said to the king of Israel, "Please inquire for the word of the Lord today."⁶ Then the king of Israel gathered the prophets together, about four hundred men, and said to them, "Shall I go against Ramoth Gilead to fight, or shall I refrain? "So they said, "Go up, for the Lord will deliver *it* into the hand of the king."⁷ And Jehoshaphat said, "*Is there* not still a prophet of the Lord here, that we may inquire of Him?"⁸ So the king of Israel said to

Jehoshaphat, "*There is* still one man, Micaiah the son of Imlah, by whom we may inquire of the Lord; but I hate him, because he does not prophesy good concerning me, but evil."

1 Samuel 9:9
Amplified Bible
⁹ Formerly in Israel, when a man went to inquire of God, he would say, "Come, let us go to the seer"

The inquirer should not become dependent on the prophet. God wants the inquirer to develop their own relationship with the Lord and receive revelation from him directly. The prophet should encourage the inquirer to do this and not become co-dependent on the prophet. The prophet should not be a replacement for God in the inquirer's life.

Myth
You should believe everything the prophet prophesies because a prophet is always accurate.

Truth
A true prophet can prophesy falsely. This happens if the revelation the prophet gets is from their flesh or the enemy. The prophet Samuel was in the flesh when he thought that Eliab, Jesse's son should be anointed as King. It was David who God chose to be king.

1 Samuel 16: 1-6
The Lord said to Samuel, "How long will you grieve for Saul, when I have rejected him as king over Israel? Fill your horn with oil and go; I will send you to Jesse the Bethlehemite, for

I have chosen a king for Myself among his sons." ² But Samuel said, "How can I go? When Saul hears *about it*, he will kill me." And the Lord said, "Take a heifer from the herd with you and say, 'I have come to sacrifice to the Lord.' ³ You shall invite Jesse to the sacrifice, and I will show you what you shall do [after that]; and you shall anoint for Me the one whom I designate." ⁴ So Samuel did what the Lord said, and came to Bethlehem. And the elders of the city came trembling to meet him and said, "Do you come in peace?" ⁵ And he said, "In peace; I have come to sacrifice to the Lord. Consecrate yourselves and come with me to the sacrifice." He also consecrated Jesse and his sons and invited them to the sacrifice. ⁶ So it happened, when they had come, he looked at Eliab [the eldest son] and thought, "Surely the Lord's anointed is before Him." ⁷ But the Lord said to Samuel, "Do not look at his appearance or at the height of his stature, because I have rejected him. For the Lord sees not as man sees; for man looks at the outward appearance, but the Lord looks at the heart.

When a prophet prophesies something that is false, that prophecy must be discerned and rejected immediately by the recipient of the prophecy or they will falsely hope that the prophecy will come to pass. Detect and reject all false prophecies.

Jeremiah 23:25-27
"I have heard what the prophets have said who prophesy lies in My name, saying, 'I have dreamed, I have dreamed! who try to make My people forget My name by their dreams which everyone tells his neighbor, as their fathers forgot My name for Baal.

Jeremiah 23:32
Behold, I am against those who prophesy false dreams," says the LORD, "and tell them, and cause My people to err by their lies and by their recklessness. Yet I did not send them or command them; therefore they shall not profit this people at all," says the LORD.

Deuteronomy 13:1-5
"If there arises among you a prophet or a dreamer of dreams, and he gives you a sign or a wonder, you shall not listen to the words of that prophet or that dreamer of dreams, for the LORD your God is testing you to know whether you love the LORD your God with all your heart and with all your soul. But that prophet or that dreamer of dreams shall be put to death, because he has spoken in order to turn you away from the LORD your God, who brought you out of the land of Egypt and redeemed you from the house of bondage, to entice you from the way in which the LORD your God commanded you to walk. So you shall put away the evil from your midst.

There are also false prophets who appear to be receiving revelation from the Lord, but they are prophesying out of a spirit of divination. Satan counterfeits everything in the body of Christ.

Matthew 7:15-16
[15] "Beware of false prophets, who come to you in sheep's clothing, but inwardly they are ravenous wolves. [16] You will know them by their fruits. Do men gather grapes from thornbushes or figs from thistles? [17] Even so, every good tree bears good fruit, but a bad tree bears bad fruit. [18] A good tree cannot bear bad fruit, nor *can* a bad tree bear good fruit.

Matthew 24: 24
[24] For false christs and false prophets will rise and show great signs and wonders to deceive, if possible, even the elect.

Myth
The prophet should always release the revelation the Lord downloads to him.

Truth
If the Holy Spirit leads the prophet to release the revelation from the Lord, he then takes that revelation and prophesies it to an individual or a corporate body (Church, organization, government, group etc.). If the Holy Spirit does not direct the prophet to release that revelation, he must not do so. If the prophet is directed by the Lord to release it, he must do it in the exact timing of the Lord. The prophet should always ask the Lord what He wants him to do with the revelation.

Chapter 13
Waging war with Prophecies

Before you can wage war with prophecies and divine revelation, you must first be absolutely positive that the prophecy or revelation is from the Lord. Waging war over false prophecies will not work. You can only wage war over authentic prophecies. Once you know with surety that the Lord has spoken, you can then wage war with the prophecy.

When an authentic prophetic word is released, the enemy wages war against the prophecy because he does not want it to happen. He strategically deploys his evil forces to intercept the promises of God released in the spiritual realm so that they cannot manifest in the earthly realm. The enemy uses guerrilla warfare tactics. Guerrilla is a Spanish word, and is derived from the word *guerra* which means war.

Guerrilla warfare is a method of irregular warfare where a small groups of combatants, such as paramilitary unit (rebels), armed civilians, or irregulars, use military tactics including ambushes, sabotage, raids, petty warfare, hit-and-run tactics, and mobility, to fight larger regular and authentic military forces. Guerrilla tactics focus on avoiding head-on confrontations with enemy armies, but instead engage in skirmishes (clashes) with the goal of exhausting adversaries and forcing them to withdraw. Lacking the numerical strength and weapons to oppose a regular army in the field, guerrillas avoid pitched battles. Instead, they operate from bases established in remote and inaccessible terrain, such as forests, mountains, and jungles. Guerrilla tactics are those of harassment. Striking swiftly and unexpectedly, they raid enemy supply depots and installations, ambush patrols and supply convoys, and cut communication lines, hoping thereby to disrupt enemy activities and to capture equipment and supplies for their own use. Because of their mobility, the dispersal of their forces into small groups, and their ability to disappear among the civilian population, guerrillas are extremely difficult to detect and capture (CIA Report: Guerrilla Warfare, 2019).

Satan is the evil mastermind behind spiritual guerrilla warfare. His forces are smaller in number and strength than God's massive and powerful army. The army of the Lord is authentic and is led by God himself, the Great I Am and the Commander in Chief. God is fighting with you and for you. His angelic hosts are also fighting with you and for you.

Deuteronomy 20:1
[1]"When you go out to battle against your enemies, and see horses and chariots and people more numerous than you, do not be afraid of them; for the Lord your God is with you.

God is omnipotent (all powerful). He is omnipresent (everywhere). He is Omniscient(He Knows all things). Satan is not omnipotent (all powerful). He is not Omnipresent - he cannot be everywhere at the same time. He is not Omniscient (all knowing). He is a created being – created by God. He is not God!! He and his army cannot be everywhere, but his evil forces are strategically deployed throughout the earth. Satan has some power, but we have been given **all** power over him by the Almighty God.

Luke 10: 19
[19] Behold, I give you the authority to trample on serpents and scorpions, and over all the power of the enemy, and nothing shall by any means hurt you.

Satanic forces engage in skirmishes with the goal of exhausting prophets and other Christians and forcing them to withdraw. They operate from the air, land and sea.

Ephesians 6:12
[[12]For we do not wrestle against flesh and blood, but against principalities, against powers, against the rulers of the darkness of this age, against spiritual hosts of wickedness in the heavenly places.

Satan has a hierarchy of demonic forces. A hierarchy is a system in which people or things are put at various levels or ranks according to their importance. Satan's hierarchy of demons is as follows:

1. Spiritual hosts of wickedness in heavenly places
2. Principalities that work in different regions
3. Powers and rulers of darkness of this age

Spiritual hosts of wickedness in heavenly places.
These are Satan's forces in the air that govern, dictate, instruct and direct the evil forces on the ground. The phrase "heavenly places" is derived from the Greek word *epouranios*, which means "the sphere of spiritual activities." The heavenly places is a sphere of spiritual activities - both angelic and demonic.

Principalities
A principality is the territory or jurisdiction of a prince. Satan has divided the world into principalities. Satan has placed a

prince over each principality. The prince of the principality of Persia is mentioned in Daniel 10. Satan's principalities work in different regions.

Powers and rulers of darkness of this age
These are two categories of demons which are at work in the social, political, and cultural systems of the world. Satan works on a national level influencing governments and nations. There are specific demons assigned to governments and seats of power (capitols).

The enemy harasses and oppresses Christians. They strike swiftly and unexpectedly. They raid our supply (God's provision to his children). They set up ambushes (surprise attacks by people lying in wait in a concealed position). They try to cut off communication between God and His children. His agents (witches and warlocks) infiltrate Churches and pose as Christians, making them difficult to detect and capture (arrest).

The enemy's actions are illegal and violate the prophetic word (the promises of God). A promise is "a legally binding declaration that gives the person to whom it is made, the **right** to expect or to claim the performance or forbearance of a specified act" (Merriam Webster, 2003). When God gives us His Word, it is legally binding. He has to perform it. He is legally bound to keeping His Word.

> **Hebrews 6:18**
> That by two **immutable** things, in which it was impossible for God to lie, we might have a strong consolation, who have fled for refuge to lay hold upon the hope set before us:

Immutable means not capable of or susceptible to change
Numbers 23:19
God is not a man, **that he should lie**; neither the son of man, that he should repent: hath he said, and shall he not do it? or hath he spoken, and shall he not make it good?

When the devil tries to stop the prophecies from manifesting, he is directly opposing the will of the Lord, and is therefore illegal and must be resisted, arrested and prosecuted for his crime.

Waging war with prophecies

Enter the Courts of Heaven

Just as there are courts in the earthly realm, so too there are courts in Heaven. God, the supreme Judge, creates, executes and enforces laws, and sits on the seat of judgment where he executes judgments and sentences against law breakers. Armed with authentic prophecies and the promises in the Logos (the Bible), enter and approach the Courts of Heaven. Drag everyone that is troubling you and is fighting against what God has promised you into the courts of heaven. Drag Satan, his demonic spirits, witches, warlocks, Christians and the unsaved into the courts of Heaven. Present your case to God. You must have prepared your case before entering the Courts of Heaven to plead your case. Prepare by writing down all the promises God gave you, written and spoken. Search the Bible and find his promises. Remember past Rhema words, prophecies, and words He personally spoke to you. Write each one down. Present and plead your case before God in detail. Remind God of his promises. Base it on the following foundation:

Matthew: 7:11
If you then, being evil, know how to give good gifts to your children, how much more will your Father who is in heaven give good things to those who ask Him!

Numbers 23:19
[19] "God *is* not a man, that He should lie,
Nor a son of man, that He should repent.
Has He said, and will He not do?
Or has He spoken, and will He not make it good?

Satan is extremely legalistic. He searches for every violation of God's laws, with the goal of executing harsh punishments for sin on those who violate God's laws. Satan knows and understands that God is the Supreme judge and is bound to uphold His laws. God is bound by his Word and is no respecter pf persons. He shows no partiality.

Knowing this Biblical truth, Satan looks for every opportunity to approach God to accuse Christians when they sin and remind God that their sin must be punished and His promises to them must be revoked or delayed.

Revelation 12:10
[10] Then I heard a loud voice saying in heaven, "Now salvation, and strength, and the kingdom of our God, and the power of His Christ have come, for the accuser of our brethren, who accused them before our God day and night, has been cast down.

Satan will even accuse a righteous man as he did with Job.

Job 1: 6-12

⁶ Now there was a day when the sons of God came to present themselves before the Lord, and Satan also came among them. ⁷ And the Lord said to Satan, "From where do you come?" So Satan answered the Lord and said, "From going to and fro on the earth, and from walking back and forth on it." ⁸ Then the Lord said to Satan, "Have you considered My servant Job, that *there is* none like him on the earth, a blameless and upright man, one who fears God and shuns evil?" ⁹ So Satan answered the Lord and said, "Does Job fear God for nothing? ¹⁰ Have You not [made a hedge around him, around his household, and around all that he has on every side? You have blessed the work of his hands, and his possessions have increased in the land. ¹¹ But now, stretch out Your hand and touch all that he has, and he will surely curse You to Your face!" ¹² And the Lord said to Satan, "Behold, all that he has *is* in your power; only do not lay a hand on his *person*." So Satan went out from the presence of the Lord.

An accuser is someone who claims that someone has committed an offence or done something wrong. As you stand before the courts of heaven and present your case, God then judges your case and if you are blameless before God, the Most High Judge, you must receive the promises. If you are guilty, you can repent and confess your sins and still receive what the Lord has promised.

1 John 1: 9

⁹ If we confess our sins, He is faithful and just to forgive us *our* sins and to cleanse us from all unrighteousness.

1 John 1:9
Amplified Bible
⁹ If we [freely] admit that we have sinned *and* confess our sins, He is faithful and just [true to His own nature and promises], and will forgive our sins and cleanse us *continually* from all unrighteousness [our wrongdoing, everything not in conformity with His will and purpose].

God will always rule in favor of the blameless person and uphold his laws (promises) on the matter presented before him. God will execute vengeance and punishment on the enemy for violating his laws. Ask God to execute his judgment on the enemy and issue a divine restraining order against him. A restraining order, also known as a protective order or non-harassment order, are court orders executed by a judge at the end of criminal proceedings to prevent the perpetrator (the offender) from causing harm to another person. A restraining order puts restrictions on the offender, for the purpose of stopping them from causing any further harm to the victim.

God will also execute his judgment (not ours) on people who are troubling you and fighting against what God has promised you.

Romans 12:19
Amplified Bible
¹⁹ Beloved, never avenge yourselves, but leave the way open for God's wrath [and His judicial righteousness]; for it is written [in Scripture], "Vengeance is Mine, I will repay," says the Lord.

2 Thessalonians 1:6
⁶ *it is* a righteous thing with God to repay with tribulation those who trouble you.

Exodus 22:18
¹⁸ Thou shalt not allow a witch to live.

Prophetic decrees and declarations
The word decree means: a ruling, a law. God's decrees are his laws, written, spoken and revealed. God directed decrees are rulings and laws that God directs the prophet to establish. Use God's decrees and God directed decrees and declare what God has spoken. A declaration, is "a formal or explicit statement or announcement" (Dictionary.com, 2013). To declare something is to proclaim it, pronounce it and release it into the air (the atmosphere). When you declare the decree, you are releasing it into the ears of the prince of the power of the air, Satan!

Ephesians 2:1-2
² And you He made alive, who were dead in trespasses and sins, ² in which you once walked according to the course of this world, according to **the prince of the power of the air, the spirit who now works in the sons of disobedience,** *[who fight against the purposes of God]*.

As you declare the decrees of the Lord, it also establishes and builds up your faith.

Romans 10:17
¹⁷ So then faith *comes* by hearing, and hearing by the word of God.

God's decrees (laws) cannot be overturned. In the book of Esther, for example, the King had made a decree to destroy all the Jews, but when Esther found favor with the King, he could not reverse the decree but instead had to issue a new decree. **Esther 3: 9-12, Esther 8: 7 -12.**

Three Way Attack

The historic "Fight Them on the Beaches" speech was delivered by the British Prime Minister Winston Churchill to the House of Commons of the Parliament of the United Kingdom on 4 June 1940 during World War 2. In part of his speech, Churchill said -"We shall fight on the beaches, we shall fight on the landing grounds, we shall fight in the fields and in the streets, we shall fight in the hills; we shall never surrender" (Churchill, 1940). The same tactics must be applied to the enemy. In a three way attack, the enemy is attacked by "air, land and sea". This is done by setting up three teams who will simultaneously attack the enemy from all sides. This is called a bombardment. A bombardment is a siege. A siege is "a continuous attack on a fortified position, usually by artillery, or surrounding and isolating it in an attempt to compel a surrender" (Dictionary.com, 2013). One of the Hebrew words for bombard is tsuwr (*pronounced tsoor)* which means to cramp; to confine; to assault; to beset; to besiege; to bind (up) ; to distress; to lay siege and to put up in bags.

In a bombardment, the three teams simultaneously do the following:

- Team One cries out to God in intercession.
- Team Two wages spiritual warfare against the enemy.
- Team Three worships God

Chapter 14
Prophetic Teams & Prophetic Presbytery

Prophetic Teams

A prophetic team is made up of prophets and prophetic Christians. The team does not have to have prophets only. Any prophetic Christian who can prophesy can be on a prophetic team. A prophetic team prophesies to individuals and groups. As with every team, unity and teamwork is mandatory for the team to function effectively. A prophetic team should be led by a seasoned prophet who has a strong prophetic anointing. The prophet should be the first person to prophesy to the person as this releases a strong impartation to others on the team, and helps them to prophesy accurately and quickly. When someone is in the presence of a prophet who has a strong prophetic anointing, the Spirit of God can move on that person and cause him or her to prophesy.

> **1 Sam 10: 1-6**
> ¹Then Samuel took a flask of oil and poured *it* on his head, and kissed him and said: "*Is it* not
> because the Lord has anointed you commander over His inheritance?

² When you have departed from me today, you will find two men by Rachel's tomb in the territory of Benjamin at Zelzah; and they will say to you, 'The donkeys which you went to look for have been found. And now your father has ceased caring about the donkeys and is worrying about you, saying, "What shall I do about my son?" ' ³ Then you shall go on forward from there and come to the terebinth tree of Tabor. There three men going up to God at Bethel will meet you, one carrying three young goats, another carrying three loaves of bread, and another carrying a skin of wine. ⁴ And they will greet you and give you two *loaves* of bread, which you shall receive from their hands. ⁵ After that you shall come to the hill of God where the Philistine garrison *is*. And it will happen, when you have come there to the city, that you will meet a group of prophets coming down from the high place with a stringed instrument, a tambourine, a flute, and a harp before them; and they will be prophesying. ⁶ Then the Spirit of the Lord will come upon you, and you will prophesy with them and be turned into another man.

1 Sam 10: 9-11

⁹ So it was, when he had turned his back to go from Samuel, that God [gave him another heart; and all those signs came to pass that day. ¹⁰ When they came there to the hill, there was a group of prophets to meet him; then the Spirit of God came upon him, and he prophesied among them. ¹¹ And it happened, when all who knew him formerly saw that he indeed prophesied among the prophets, that the people said to one another, "What *is* this *that* has come upon the son of Kish? *Is* Saul also among the prophets?"

The prophetic team must flow together. They must prophesy one at a time. Each person on the team must wait until someone finishes prophesying before they release their prophecy.

1 Corinthians 14:40
Let all things be done decently and in order.

The prophetic team must work in tandem (alongside each other; one behind another). A team that is working "in tandem" means they are working together, especially well and closely. A tandem is a type of bicycle that is made for two people.

Illustration by Vecteezy.com

"A tandem lets two riders of different abilities cycle together without anyone getting left behind. Tandems have two seats, one behind the other. The front rider, called the pilot or captain, controls the steering, the brakes and the gears. The rear rider, called the stoker, helps to pedal. Because of the extra weight and power on a tandem compared to a solo bike, it's easiest to control if the heavier, stronger rider is the pilot" (We are cycling UK, 2021).

The prophetic team must observe all prophetic protocols and outlined in Chapter 5. Two of the most important prophetic protocols are :

1. **Do not speak or pray when someone else is prophesying.**
The person cannot hear if you speak or pray when another person is prophesying. Remember that it is the Lord speaking through the other prophet and if you speak or pray when the prophecy is being released, you are in interrupting God.

2. **Prophetic Plagiarism**
Prophets who are ministering on a team, often get the same revelation for a person, place, organization, church or other entity. When the first prophet prophesies what you also got from the Lord, still prophesy it. But you should always confirm a prophecy given by someone else by prophesying it also but confirming what the other prophet/prophets said. Start the prophecy by saying "I confirm what prophet so and so said. I also got the same thing" **And you can then reiterate it!!** Do not claim a prophesy another prophet prophesied as your own. This is called prophetic plagiarism. Plagiarism is "presenting someone else's work or ideas as your own, with or without their consent, by incorporating it into your work without full acknowledgement" (Oxford Dictionary, 2021).

Prophetic Presbytery
The word presbytery in Greek is <u>presbuterion</u> *(pronounced pres-boo-ter'-ee-on)* which means the order of elders. Unlike the prophetic team that consists of prophets and prophetic Christians, the prophetic presbytery is made up of the elders

of a local Church. Prophetic presbytery is when the presbyters (elders) lay hands on and prophesy over selected believers to speak the will of God over them, impart spiritual gifts to them, at their ordinations and release them into their ministries.

1 Timothy 4:14
Amplified Bible
¹⁴ Do not neglect the spiritual gift within you, [that special endowment] which was intentionally bestowed on you [by the Holy Spirit] through prophetic utterance when the elders laid their hands on you [at your ordination].

Questions:
What is the difference between a prophetic team and a prophetic presbytery?

_____
_____
_____
_____
_____
_____
_____
_____
_____

Chapter 15
The Prophet's authority

Authority means: power to influence or command thought, opinion, or behavior. The prophet must first know what authority God has given to them and how to use that authority. The prophet must not misuse that authority especially for personal gain.

Firstly, the prophet, along with all other Christians, has the authority of the King of Kings over all the power of the enemy.

> **Luke 10:19**
> Behold, I give you the authority to trample on serpents and scorpions, and over all the power of the enemy, and nothing shall by any means hurt you.

The prophet has also been given the keys to the Kingdom of Heaven. When someone gives you a key to their house, it signifies they trust you and have given you the authority and power to use that key to enter their house. The keys to the Kingdom of God is the power to bind and loose.

> **Matthew 16:19**
> [19] And I will give you the keys of the kingdom of heaven, and whatever you bind on earth will be bound in heaven, and whatever you loose on earth will be loosed in heaven.

To bind means: to tie up, to put restraints and fetters on (Dictionary.com, 2013). Restraints keep a violent person in a way that prevents them from moving freely.

A fetter is a chain or manacle, typically placed around the ankles, which is used to restrain a prisoner. To loose means to set free, to release something. When you bind the spiritual forces of the enemy always loose (replace it with) the spiritual forces or attributes of the Lord.

Examples of binding and loosing.

Bind the spirit of:	Loose
Fear	Faith
Defeat	Victory
Sorrow	Joy
Divination	Prophecy
Witchcraft	Humility Submission Repentance Love of God Compliance
Confusion	The Mind of Christ God's Original Plan and Purpose Peace Love Soundness of Mind Order
Quitting	Staying Strength Courage Whole Mindedness

The prophet must implement God's authority and bind the enemy by putting restraints on them to keep them in a place of immobility where they cannot move freely. When the prophet, who is the mouthpiece of God, restrains the enemy he is controlling his actions and behavior by force, in order to stop them from doing something.

James 4:7
7 Therefore submit to God. Resist the devil and he will flee from you.

Resist means to fight against something or someone that is attacking you; to refuse to accept or be changed by something or someone. The prophet must fight offensively and not defensively against the enemy and refuse to accept or allow the enemy to change him or change their circumstances and destiny. The prophet must also use the power to bind and loose over Churches, governments, nations, evil laws, and other organizations and events. Always bind backlash and retaliation before and after engaging the enemy in warfare.

Secondly, the prophet is a spokesman for God and prophesies in God's name and by his authority. The prophet has the authority of the Lord to speak and act in his name. The prophet ranks second in the Church, and therefore carries a greater authority than teacher, evangelist, pastor and all other Christians with the exception of the Apostle.

1 Corinthians 12:28
28 And God has appointed these in the church: first apostles, second prophets, third teachers, after that miracles, then gifts of healings, helps, administrations, varieties of tongues.

Because of the rank and authority of the prophet, and the fact that he is God's spokesman, God admonishes people to honor and respect the prophet.

Romans 13:1-6
[1] Let every soul be subject to the governing authorities. For there is no authority except from God, and the authorities that exist are appointed by God. [2] Therefore whoever resists the authority resists the ordinance of God, and those who resist will [a]bring judgment on themselves. [3] For rulers are not a terror to good works, but to evil. Do you want to be unafraid of the authority? Do what is good, and you will have praise from the same. [4] For he is God's minister to you for good. But if you do evil, be afraid; for he does not bear the sword in vain; for he is God's minister, an avenger to execute wrath on him who practices evil. [5] Therefore you must be subject, not only because of wrath but also for conscience' sake. [6] For because of this you also pay taxes, for they are God's ministers attending continually to this very thing.

1 Chronicles 16:22
"Do not touch My anointed ones,
And do My prophets no harm."

God honors his prophets and expects other do so as well. Whoever honors a prophet they will receive a prophet's reward.

Matthew 10:41-42
[41] He who receives a prophet in the name of a prophet shall receive a prophet's reward.

The prophet must be honored but not worshipped. Honoring a prophet is to treat the prophet with high respect and great esteem. Worship must be rendered to God only. To worship anyone or anything is idolatry. Both Apostle Peter and an angel refused to be worshipped.

Acts 10:25-26
[25] As Peter was coming in, Cornelius met him and fell down at his feet and worshiped *him*. [26] But Peter lifted him up, saying, "Stand up; I myself am also a man."

Revelation 22:8-9
Amplified Bible
[8] I, John, am the one who heard and saw these things. And when I heard and saw them, I fell down to worship before the feet of the angel who showed me these things. [9] But he said to me, "Do not do that. I am a fellow servant with you and your brothers the prophets and with those who heed *and* remember [the truths contained in] the words of this book. Worship God."

Questions:
What is prophetic authority?

_____

_____

_____

_____

_____

What are the keys of the kingdom of heaven?

What are some of the ways to honor a prophet?

Chapter 16
Prophetic Interpretation

There are two types of prophecies: literal and symbolic. Literal prophecies do not require an interpretation, but symbolic prophecies do.

Literal Prophecies
Literal prophecies are exactly as they are spoken. They are not cryptic. Cryptic means "expressing something in a mysterious or indirect way so that it is difficult to understand" (Dictionary.com, 2013). A literal prophecy is not an enigma. You don't have to decipher it, decode it or interpret its meaning.

Symbolic Prophecies
Symbolic prophecies require an interpretation. You have to discern what the Lord is really saying. God said it. But you must interpret it. Interpret means to "translate what someone is saying in one language into another language so that someone else can understand it" (Dictionary.com, 2013). God often speaks in a different language to the one you speak and understand. It is therefore important to understand God's language.

God's Language	Man's Interpretation	What God really means
I will answer your petitions	I will grant you your requests	The answer can be a yes or a no
You are called to be a Moses	You will not enter the promised Land	You are called to be a mighty deliverer
I am giving you new garments	I am getting new clothes	New life. New season. I am cleaning up your life,
I am giving you wisdom	I am going to solve everyone's problems I will be one of the smartest persons on the earth	You will have difficult situations that you cannot solve which will require God's wisdom
You are called to hurting people	I will have a great anointing to heal the brokenhearted.	Hurt people hurt people. You will need more great love and compassion to deal with them. Difficult people will come.
Patience	I will persevere in difficult situations.	Tribulation will come. Tribulation produces patience. Romans 5:1-5

Great victory	Great victory	A major battle is coming, but you will be victorious.
You are an overcomer	I will overcome every trial	You will experience many trials and tribulations
You are called to greatness	I will be known by many people	You will have seasons of humility

1 Corinthians 13:9-12

⁹ For we know in part and we prophesy in part. ¹⁰ But when that which is perfect has come, then that which is in part will be done away. ¹¹ When I was a child, I spoke as a child, I understood as a child, I thought as a child; but when I became a man, I put away childish things. ¹² For now we see in a mirror, dimly, but then face to face. Now I know in part, but then I shall know just as I also am known.

Questions:

What is the difference between a literal prophecy and a symbolic prophecy?

_____
_____
_____
_____
_____
_____

Why does God speak symbolically?

About the Author

Lisa Sims is an apostle and prophet. She and her husband are founders of Across the Globe Ministries. Apostle Lisa has been in ministry for almost 30 years and has trained, ordained and commissioned men and women who are called to the Office of the Prophet. Apostle Lisa has raised up a company of prophets like the Old Testament prophets who were holy and delivered accurate and detailed prophecies.

Apostle Lisa who is a native of Trinidad and Tobago, lived in the United States of America for 27 years. She is the founder of several ministries in the USA, Trinidad and Tobago and the United Kingdom. Apostle Lisa travels worldwide to advance the Kingdom of God through preaching the gospel with signs, wonders and miracles, training, equipping, mobilizing and mentoring God's mighty end-time army to reach the lost. She plants, strengthens and oversees churches and ministries, and mentors and oversees five-fold ministers and other Christians.

Apostle Lisa, who is affectionately called Apostle Mom, is a spiritual mom to many sons and daughters worldwide. She is a nurturing and compassionate woman of God who has ministered healing and deliverance to thousands of people in many nations. Apostle Lisa has a tremendous compassion for abused, hurting and abandoned women and children, , a powerful anointing to heal the brokenhearted and the mentally, emotionally and physically sick and to deliver those who are oppressed with demonic spirits, having herself overcome sexual, emotional and physical abuse both as a child and as an adult. Many of them have gone on to become productive men and women. Some have become ministers of the gospel, teachers, authors, entrepreneurs, and one a politician. Lisa has also counseled and rehabilitated prisoners and juvenile offenders in jails, prisons and juvenile centers.

Apostle Lisa's Contact Information
info@acrosstheglobeministries.org
lisaharrissims@gmail.com

Lisa Sims Biography
No One Would Love Her
Available on Amazon

I was beaten, drugged and sexually molested by my father. My mother hated me for it and emotionally and physically abused me and treated me as though I was her husband's (my father's) lover! My horrific and painful abuse drove me into the arms of men who I thought would love me, but who also abused me, beat me and hated me. My painful years of abuse began as a very young child and lasted throughout many of my adult years. I tried to kill myself, but I lived. I lived and found and experienced God's love for me and His purpose for my life. I overcame the pain of abuse, rejection and feelings of worthlessness and despair through God's love and His healing and deliverance. I am now a minister, life coach and counselor, and minister healing and deliverance to countless abused and battered women and children throughout the world. My story of abuse will bring hope and healing to you. Everyone who has read has said that they simply could not put my book down and that it brought healing and deliverance to them as they read it. My story will captivate you, and you will want to read it again and again. You can buy my book on Amazon.

References

Churchill, W. (1940, June 4). *Winston Churchill.* Retrieved from International Churchill Society: https://winstonchurchill.org/resources/speeches/1940-the-finest-hour/we-shall-fight-on-the-beaches/

(2019). *CIA Report: Guerrilla Warfare.* CIA.

Dictionary. (2013, January 26). Retrieved from http://dictionary.reference.com/browse/realm

Dictionary.com. (2013, January 26). Retrieved from http://dictionary.reference.com/browse/realm

Easton's Bible Dictionary. (2021, April 1). Retrieved from Easton's Bible Dictionary: https://eastonsbibledictionary.org/3006-Prophet.php

Hamilton, J. (2013). *The Nature of Our Enemy.*

Henson, S. (2009). *The Pride The Rebellion and Jezebel.*

Merriam Webster. (2003, February 1). Retrieved from https://www.merriam-webster.com/

Oxford Dictionary. (2021, April 25). Retrieved from Oxford University Dictionary: https://www.ox.ac.uk/

Strong's Concordance with Hebrew and Greek Lexicon. (2021, April 1). Retrieved from Strong's Lexicon: https://www.eliyah.com/lexicon.html

Vine's Expository Dictionary of New Testament Words. (2021, March 25). Retrieved from Vines: https://studybible.info/vines/

We are cycling UK. (2021, March 2). Retrieved from https://www.cyclinguk.org/article/cycling-guide/guide-tandems

www.ingramcontent.com/pod-product-compliance
Lightning Source LLC
Chambersburg PA
CBHW072053110526
44590CB00018B/3159